One Lord, One Church,
One Task

One Lord, One Church, One Task

2000 Keswick Ministry

Edited by Hilary Price

OM
publishing

First published in 2000 by OM Publishing

06 05 04 03 02 01 00   7 6 5 4 3 2 1

OM publishing is an imprint of Paternoster Publishing,
PO Box 300, Carlisle, Cumbria CA3 0QS, UK
and Paternoster Publishing USA
Box 1047, Waynesboro, GA 30830-2047
www.paternoster-publishing.com

British Library Cataloguing in Publication Data

A catalogue record for this book is available from the British Library

ISBN 1-85078-365-9

Cover design by Campsie
Typeset by WestKey Ltd., Falmouth, Cornwall
Printed in Great Britain by Cox and Wyman,
Cardiff Road, Reading, Berkshire, RG1 8EX

Contents

The Bible Readings

Studies in 1 Corinthians 1–4
by Dr John Stott

Studies in Nehemiah
by Jonathan Lamb

The Addresses

Introduction by the Chairman of the 2000 Convention

One Lord, One Church, One Task

In his recent lectures on globalization, Anthony Giddens used the example of a friend who was studying village life in a remote area of Central Africa. She was invited to a local home for an evening's entertainment and went expecting to find out about the traditional pastimes of this isolated community. Instead the occasion turned out to be a viewing of *Basic Instinct*, a film that at that point hadn't reached the cinemas in London.

All of us have become familiar with the idea of the 'global village'. The communications revolution has changed our perception of the world we live in. As Christians, of course, we rejoice in the fact that we belong to the one family, God's international community, but this side of heaven we have few opportunities to experience its reality.

For two weeks in the Lake District town of Keswick, in the summer of 2000, something like the global village prevailed. With the 125th anniversary theme of *One World, One Church, One Task*, record crowds arrived from around the world, including representatives from 'Keswick Conventions' from other continents as well as national leaders and missionaries. Sharing a common devotion to Jesus Christ, they joined with thousands from throughout Britain to rejoice in the truth that He is the Saviour of the world.

The teaching given at Keswick, reflected in these pages, not only emphasized the realities of the gospel but was given a strong global emphasis through the ministry of several speakers from other parts of the world, including the passionate call to honour Christ from Ann Graham Lotz, the international concerns and evangelistic fervour of Luis Palau, the thought-provoking reflections of Vinoth Ramachandra and the energetic exhortations to mission from George Verwer, who admitted he was more of a 'spiritual hand-grenade thrower' than an expositer and said, 'If world mission isn't a priority in your life and your church, you need to repent.'

It was particularly heartening that an event that is entering its 126th year can sustain a commitment to its core values whilst introducing change in line with the century we have now entered. The new 'K2' programme entitled 'The world is not enough', for those in their 20s and 30s, the commitment to greater accessibility for all of God's people including those with learning difficulties, the sustained development of work amongst young people, the growing numbers of families, the deployment of various media to spread the Word still further, whether through Premier Radio, Sky Digital, the Internet, BBC *Songs of Praise* – all of these represent the expanding ministry of the Keswick Convention to a new generation and a growing global audience.

For all of these good things we thank God.

We hope that as you read these pages you will capture something of the flavour of the event and will renew your commitment to the One Lord who has saved us, the One Church to which we belong, and the One Task of proclaiming Jesus Christ in today's world.

Jonathan Lamb, Chairman of the Convention Council

Editor's Introduction

Keswick 2000 was a special event – it celebrated 125 years of the Convention. People came from all over the world to take part and thankfully they seemed to bring the sunshine with them! Those of us who live locally know that sadly, they also seemed to take it away again! The numbers were up on last year, reaching over 10,000, and there was a wonderful atmosphere as people of all ages, from many different countries, in a great variety of colours and costumes mixed to learn about and actually illustrate the theme, *One Lord, One Church, One Task*. What wonderful memories of fellowship in the sun.

However, the holidays come to an end and the start of the autumn school term has now become synonymous for me with getting down to work on editing the Keswick Book. Once again I consider it a privilege to listen to a selection of the messages from the two weeks and to shuffle them into some sort of order that will truly represent the speakers. I am sorry to have to leave out some wonderful stories which make excellent illustrations (and even those that don't, but are just good stories!), but not there is not room to print every word spoken from the platform.

I have followed the same basic guidelines as usual. All Bible references that were included in the talks are included in the text and unless specified, the New International Version has been used throughout. When speakers paraphrase, the reference is preceded by 'cf.', just in case you start thinking,

'It doesn't say that in my Bible!' Capitalization is used for the persons of the Trinity unless within a direct quotation from the NIV. I would encourage you to read the messages with access to an open Bible so that you not only hear the speakers' individual styles and voices, but ultimately you hear God speak to you personally, no longer in the sunshine, in the tent at Keswick, but wherever you may be.

Hilary Price, Keswick Volume Editor

The Bible Readings

Studies in 1 Corinthians 1–4

Calling Christian Leaders

Corinthian Studies in Gospel, Church and Ministry

by Dr John Stott

1. The Ambiguity of the Church
1 Corinthians 1:1–17

Introduction

I have entitled this series, 'Calling Christian Leaders!' and I think all of us, to some degree, are in leadership roles, whether as parents or teachers, pastors or leaders in our local church, hence the subtitle, 'Corinthian studies in Gospel, Church and Ministry'. Let me introduce the topic. I reckon that one of the great things that unites us in Keswick is that we are all committed to the church. Of course we are all committed to Christ – all one in Christ Jesus, but we are also committed to the body of Christ. We come from different races, countries, nations, cultures and denominations, but we are all members of that amazing phenomenon called the worldwide Christian community – at least I hope we are. I hope there is nobody present who is that bizarre anomaly, 'an un-churched Christian', because the New Testament knows nothing of such a monster. If we are committed to Christ, we must be committed to the body of Christ. The reason we are committed to the church is because God is committed to the church. His purpose, we are told in the New Testament, is not just to save isolated individuals and so perpetuate our loneliness, God's purpose is to 'build the church'. Christ died for us, we are told in Titus 2, not only that we might be redeemed from all iniquity, but that He might purify for Himself a people who are enthusiastic for good works.

The image of the church, which these chapters present, is extremely ambiguous. There is a paradox at the very heart of the church: the painful tension between what the church *claims* to be and what the church *seems* to be; between the divine ideal and the human reality; between romantic talk about the bride of Christ and the very unromantic, ugly, unholy and quarrelsome people we know ourselves to be. It is a tension between our final glorious destiny in heaven and our present very inglorious performance. This is the ambiguity of the church.

The apostle describes himself as the author of the letter, and the Corinthians as the recipients of the letter. Paul, the 'apostle of Christ by the will of the God', writes to the Corinthian Christians, 'the church of God in Corinth'. So an apostle of Christ addresses a church of God and both of them are exalted, noble titles.

a) Paul's self-description (v. 1)

In nine out of the thirteen letters attributed to the apostle Paul, he identifies himself as an apostle of Christ by the will of God, by the command of God or by the commission of God. How are we to understand this word 'apostle'? It is used in three different senses in the New Testament.

Firstly, it is used once only in the New Testament of all disciples of Jesus, 'the messenger is not above the one who sent him' (Jn. 13:16). The word 'messenger' is in the Greek, *apostalos*. The messenger is not above the one who sent him. All of us have been sent into the world to share in the apostolic mission of the church and to share the good news of Jesus Christ with others.

Secondly, it is used three or four times in the New Testament of the so-called 'apostles of the churches'. Not the apostles of Christ, but the apostles of the churches – people sent out by a particular church on a particular mission. We would call them missionaries or maybe mission partners, but Paul called

Epaphroditus the *apostalos* of the church of Philippi (Phil. 2:25). He refers to him as your apostle, the man sent by you in order to minister in this case to me. In 2 Corinthians 8:23 there are people called the representatives of the churches, literally the apostles of the churches.

Thirdly, the overwhelming number of times in the New Testament, the word is applied to the twelve, to Paul who was added to their number, to James who was also added and probably that's all. They were not apostles of the churches, they were apostles of Jesus Christ and they were a unique group with the following characteristics:

a) They had been chosen, called and appointed directly by Jesus Christ, not by any human being or by any church.

b) They were eye witnesses of the historic Jesus, either of His public ministry, like the twelve for three years, or of His resurrection, like Paul. Paul could be an apostle because he had seen the risen Lord (1 Cor. 9:1). 'Am I not an apostle?' he says. 'Have I not seen Jesus our Lord?' He could not have been an apostle if he had not seen the historic Jesus.

c) They were promised a special inspiration of the Holy Spirit as we read in John 14 and 16, to remind them of what Jesus had taught them whilst on earth, and to supplement that teaching, adding to it that 'He will guide you into all truth' (Jn. 6:13). Those great promises were fulfilled in the writing of the New Testament.

It is extremely important, in these days, to hold fast to the uniqueness of the apostles of Christ and to hold their unique authority as the apostles of Christ and so the unique authority of the New Testament. The New Testament is precisely the teaching of the apostles. It is in the New Testament that their teaching has come down to us in its definitive form.

Theological liberals are sometimes brash and foolish enough to say, 'Well that was Paul's opinion, but this is my opinion. Paul was a first-century witness to Christ, but I am a twenty-first-century witness to Christ.' And they claim an authority equal to that of the apostles. Recently, an American episcopal bishop said, 'We wrote the Bible, so we can rewrite it.' Excuse me, bishop, we did not write the Bible! Biblical authors did not write in the name of the church. On the contrary, they wrote to the church in the name of God, in the case of the Old Testament prophets and in the name of Christ, in the case of the New Testament apostles. That is why we receive their teaching as the Word of God, not as the word of men but as the Word of God.

As we start in the first four chapters of 1 Corinthians, let us not wander through the text like a gardener in a herbaceous border, picking a flower here and discarding a flower there. Let us not imagine that the New Testament is a collection of the fallible opinions of fallible human beings. Let us, rather, acknowledge and receive these chapters as part of the Word of God. Let us be ready to humble ourselves under the authority of the Word of God, determined that we will listen attentively to what He has spoken, with a view to believing and obeying it. For the New Testament is the teaching of the apostles and the apostles teach the Word of God.

So much then for Paul's self-description. He had been called to be an apostle of Christ. True, he also mentioned Sosthenes, but he only calls him 'our brother'. Sosthenes was not an apostle like Paul. Indeed, I weigh my words carefully, but we need to have the courage to insist today that there are no longer any apostles in the church. There are people who could be described as having 'apostolic ministries': bishops, superintendents, pioneer missionaries, and church planters. But there are no apostles comparable to the apostle Paul, or the apostle John, or the apostle Peter and if there were, we would have to add their teaching to the New Testament. There is nobody from the Pope downwards or the Pope upwards (whichever way you would like to put it), with that authority in the church today. These are the apostles of Christ and we submit to their authority in the New Testament.

b) Paul's Description of the Corinthian Church (v. 2)

The words 'to the church of God in Corinth' sound innocent enough, at first hearing, until we reflect upon them. Is it not extraordinary that such a community should exist in such a city? The church of God in Corinth. Let's think about Corinth. Its distinction is due mainly to its strategic location on the Corinthian Isthmus, where it commanded the trade routes north-south by land and east-west by sea. It was a manufacturing city and a trading centre which hosted the famous Isthmian Games every two years. It was also a religious city. Its temple to Aphrodite dominated the Acrocorinth behind the city and its temple of Apollo stood in the very centre of the town. It was also an immoral city. To 'corinthianize', the Greek verb, meant to live an immoral life. It had political significance because it was the capital city of the Roman province of Asia. Thus Corinth was a busy, thriving, affluent and permissive city. Merchants and sailors, pilgrims and athletes, tourists and prostitutes jostled with one another in its narrow streets.

Yet, in this heathen city there lived a small group of people whom the apostle calls 'the church of God' – the divine community in the midst of the human community. Those were its two habitats simultaneously: it lived in Christ and in Corinth. It's a marvellous thought – it was like a fragrant flower growing in and out of rather smelly mud. It had two habitats – in Christ and in Corinth; two sanctities – actual and potential; and two callings – objective and subjective. God calls us to be holy and we call on God to make us holy. God calls us to be the holy people we are and we call on God to be the unique person He is according to His name. Indeed, it is only by calling upon God to be Himself, that we have any hope of becoming more truly ourselves as God intends us to be.

Fundamental, then, to New Testament Christianity is this ambiguity of the church and of salvation. We are living in between times. We are living in between the First and the Second Comings of Christ; between what He did when He first came and what He is going to do when He comes back. We are living between Kingdom come and Kingdom coming, between the 'now already' of the Kingdom inaugurated and the 'not yet' of the Kingdom yet to be consummated. And this living in between times is a key to our understanding of 1 Corinthians. The great John Newton, author of 'Amazing Grace', once said, 'I am not yet what I ought to be and I am not what I want to be. I am not what I hope to be in another world, but still I am not what I used to be. And I am, by the grace of God, I am what I am.'

Having looked at the apostle Paul, an apostle of Jesus Christ by the will of God, and at Corinth, we are now going to put the two together and see that Paul had a close, longstanding, affectionate, personal and pastoral relationship with the Corinthian church. It began in the year AD 50, when he first visited Corinth on his second missionary journey and founded the church there. If we use the three metaphors which he himself developed a little later in chapter 3, we may say that Paul planted the church; Apollos and others watered it. Paul laid the foundation of the church; others erected the superstructure on the foundation. He fathered the church; others were its guardians and its tutors. Over the years Paul visited Corinth at least three times and wrote to the church at least four times, although only two of his letters have survived.

That may have seemed a lengthy introduction, but I think we need to understand the background before we plunge into the text. Now you will notice, firstly, Paul *greets* the church (1:1–3), secondly, Paul *gives thanks* for the church (1:4–9) and thirdly, he *appeals* to the church (1:10–17). In each section, the greeting, the thanksgiving and the appeal, he singles out one essential characteristic of the Christian community. In relation to the first – *holiness*; in relation to the second – *giftedness*; and in relation to the third – *unity*. So let's look at these three.

1) Paul greets the church (1:1–3)

In his greeting he emphasizes the holiness of the church. What he has called the church of God in Corinth, he now also designates those who have been; it's a perfect tense, those who *have been* sanctified in Christ Jesus. And then he goes on to call them those who *are* called to be saints or called to be holy. The ambiguity is obvious: the church is already sanctified and it's not yet holy. Moreover, this is true of all those who, everywhere, call on the name of the Lord Jesus Christ, both their Lord and ours. So, on the one hand, the Christian community of the church of God, like Israel before it, was the holy people of God. Its members have been set apart to belong to God. He had chosen them to be His special people: that is their status, set apart and sanctified, to belong to God alone. On the other hand, as the coming chapters make clear, much unholiness lingered in the Christian community: quarrelling, pride, complacency, immorality, taking one another to court, disorders in public worship, boastfulness of spiritual gifts. This holy church of Corinth was very unholy. There is the first example of ambiguity.

2) Paul gives thanks for the church (1:4–9)

In his thanksgiving he emphasizes the giftedness of the church. In spite of its many failures he begins with this positive evaluation. Beginning at verse 4 he says, 'I always thank God for you,' and we can always thank God for one another. But what did he thank God for? First because God's grace was given to you in Christ Jesus. And that is surely a reference to their salvation, the grace of God had come to them and saved them. Next, verse 5, he gives thanks to God because in Christ you have been enriched in every way and by what he goes on to say, he is evidently thinking of their spiritual gifts, their knowledge and their ability to communicate the knowledge which they have been given. And finally, verse 6, because Paul's apostolic testimony to Christ had been confirmed in them. Christ had proved, in their own experience, to be everything which the apostle Paul said that He was. And for those things, the grace, the enrichment, the confirmation of the apostle's testimony, Paul gives thanks. In consequence, verse 7, you don't lack any spiritual gift.

It's an amazing thanksgiving to God. It sounds as if the Corinthian church was perfect, in every way enriched, in no way deficient, in other words – complete. Not, of course, that every individual Christian has all the spiritual gifts. We know that from chapter 12 in particular. A wide diversity or variety of gifts are given to different people and if you bring together all the lists of the charismata in the New Testament, there are at least twenty-one mentioned. So it isn't each individual that has all the gifts, but each local church may expect to have, collectively, all the gifts it needs. And yet, this is not the end of the story.

Even though the Corinthian church had been graced and gifted and enriched in Christ, so that they lacked nothing, they were not yet blameless. That's why they were still eagerly waiting for the revelation of our Lord Jesus Christ. In spite of everything He had given them, as a result of His First Coming, they were longing for His Second Coming, when they would become blameless. He would keep them strong until the end, and on the last day they would be blameless in His sight. How do we know that? Well, not because of our faith but because of God's faithfulness: 'Faithful is the God who called you into the fellowship of His Son Jesus Christ' (v. 9). So, one day He will perfect the fellowship into which He has already brought us. 'God called us' is a past reality; 'into the fellowship of Christ' is a present experience; 'God is faithful' is the ground of our confidence for the future. That beautiful verse 9 speaks of the past, the present and the future. So here is the second ambiguity of the church. First the church is holy, but is called to be holy. Second, the church is complete and yet it is incomplete, which is why we are eagerly waiting for the revelation of Jesus Christ.

3) Paul appeals to the Corinthian church (1:10–17)

In his appeal he emphasizes the unity of the church. Herein lies the ambiguity: this united church is also divided. The very same tension between the reality and the ideal. Let's look back to verse 2 about the unity of the church. Paul describes Corinth as *the* church of God, not the churches of God. There may have been several house churches, or house fellowships in Corinth, we don't know for certain, but he still calls it *the* church of God, one and undivided. I've no doubt God says to Himself from time to time, 'I have only one church – it is the body of Christ, it is the temple of the Holy Spirit, there *is* only one church, *My* church.' Or again, we might say as Paul does in Ephesians 4, there is only one family because there is only one Father. And there is only one body because there is only one Holy Spirit who indwells the one body. There is only one faith, one hope, one baptism because there is only one Jesus Christ in whom we have believed, for whom we are waiting in hope and into whom we have been baptized. The one Father creates the one family, the one Christ creates the one faith, hope and baptism and the one Holy Spirit creates the one body. And there is only one church to which we bear witness at Keswick. So a little later, in chapter 3, he will say, 'You are God's field, you are God's temple, you are the body of Christ.' Collective nouns which all declare the unity of the church.

But we Christians, who are one, have nevertheless succeeded in dividing from one another. We have divided the indivisible. We have made God's one and only church into many churches and we ought to be ashamed of ourselves. Like the Corinthian Christians, as Chloe's household had told Paul in verse 11, although there was one church it was torn apart by factions. Paul has given thanks for them, but now he appeals to them. He has been affirming them, but now he rebukes them. And we need to look at that.

What can we learn from his appeal? Notice first, he addresses them as brothers (vv. 10, 11), reminding them of the family of God in which all Christian people are sisters and brothers. But unfortunately, although they are all members of the family of God, they are contradicting that by their behaviour. Notice the basis of his appeal. It is in the one and only name of our Lord Jesus Christ – the name that is above every name, on which all Christian believers call (v. 2), 'the name into which we have all been baptized' (vv. 13, 15). They named human names, I belong to Paul, I belong to Peter, I belong to Apollos. But as the great Chrysostom in the fourth to fifth century, one of the fathers of the church, says in his commentary, 'Paul keeps nailing them to the Name of Christ,' diverting their attention from Paul, Apollos and Peter, to Christ – the one and only Jesus Christ.

Paul repeats his appeal in verse 10, 'that all of you agree with one another so that there be no divisions with each

other'. Already there are quarrels, but he says, 'Let there be
no divisions among you … that you may be perfectly united
in mind and in thought.' In verse 11 he goes into more
detail about being informed about their quarrels by some
members of Chloe's household, concluding in verse 12,
'What I mean is this: One of you says, "I follow Paul";
another, "I follow Apollos"; another, "I follow Cephas";
still another, "I follow Christ." '

Now there is much debate and discussion about the identity
of these different groups in the church of Corinth. Some try to
find different theologies here in contradiction with one
another. The most famous is the theory of the nineteenth-
century German theologian F.C. Baur, who was a New
Testament professor at Tübingen in Germany. He argued that
in the early church there was a fundamental opposition
between the Gentile party, headed by the apostle Paul, and the
Jewish party, headed by the apostle Peter. He interpreted the
whole of the New Testament in the light of this quarrel and
antagonism between Paul and Peter, between Gentiles and
Jews in the Christian community. He found support for his
opinion here in this passage that we are looking at. But
honestly, as we look at the text here, there is no evidence that
these groups were divided by theology or by doctrine. No,
they were divided by personalities not by principles. The
groups are separated from one another by the cult of celebrities, by pride, by jealousy, by boastfulness, of their different
church leaders, and all this deeply disturbed the apostle. He was
their brother, he calls them my sisters and brothers, he is not
their master, that they should think they belong to him. If anybody belongs to anybody in the church, he belongs to them,
they don't belong to him.

So what about the fourth slogan, 'I belong to Christ'? How
could one faction, in Corinth, possibly claim an exclusive
monopoly of the Lord Jesus? All Christians belong to Christ,
not one clique or faction within the church, and for that reason some suggest, and I myself believe this is correct, that
although the first three were watchwords in the Corinthian
church – I belong to Paul, to Apollos to Peter, the fourth was
not a fourth faction, but Paul's own indignant retort: You may

say that you belong to Paul and Peter and Apollos, but as for me, I belong to Christ and not to any human leader.

This was serious. Although the divisions were not doctrinal in origin, they had profound doctrinal implications, especially in relation to Christ, to the gospel and to baptism. To show this, the apostle asks three leading questions in verse 13, all of which demand an emphatic 'No!' as the answer.

1) Is Christ divided? J.B. Phillips translates it, 'Is there more than one Christ? Are there lots of different Christs?' C.K. Barrett translates it, 'Has Christ been shared out? Fragments of Him being distributed to different groups in the church?' No! No! No! There is only one Christ.

2) 'Was Paul crucified for you?' Are you trusting for your salvation in Paul and him crucified? Answer No! No! No! The idea is preposterous. Jesus Christ is our crucified Saviour in whom alone we have put our trust.

3) 'Were you baptized into the name of Paul?' No! No! No! Of course not! Baptism is into allegiance to Christ. We are baptized into Christ, as Romans 6 makes clear, into union with Christ in His death and resurrection. Thus you see the effect of their divisions was to undermine these essentials of the gospel. It was to deny there was only one Christ, who is the only one who died to be our Saviour, and into whose name alone we have been baptized. So clearly, the person of Christ, the cross of Christ, the name of Christ into which we have been baptized, are all at stake when the church divides. The Corinthians were insulting Christ, they were dislodging Him from His supremacy, they were replacing Him with human leaders.

Now, we move on to verses 14–17. Paul lingers on the topic of baptism. Because they were putting their emphasis in the wrong place, they were exalting the human baptizer, the person who actually did the dipping or the sprinkling, at the expense of the divine Christ into whom they had been baptized. Consequently Paul expressed his thankfulness for what he saw as the providence of God. Gordon Fee calls it, 'a simple uncalculated, historical reality namely that he had not baptized any of them'. Oh, wait a minute (having had a little lapse of memory), I did baptize Crispus the ruler of the synagogue and Gaius who became the host of the church, verse 15, so no one can say you were baptized into my name, Paul, and I did baptize 'the household of Stephanas; and beyond that I can't remember if I baptized anyone else' (v. 16), so comparatively unimportant is it, as to who does the baptizing. What matters in baptism is not the person *by* whom we were baptized but the Person *into* whom we were baptized – Jesus Christ Himself. Besides, Paul adds, verse 17, Christ had sent him, literally, Christ had apostled him, not to baptize but to evangelize.

Now Paul is not being derogatory to baptism; he knew that Jesus had instituted baptism, he knew it was an integral part of the great commission, he had not forgotten that. He had a very high view of baptism himself, as you can tell if you read Romans 6. But Paul's specialty, as an apostle of Christ, was evangelism and not baptism. He was a pioneer preacher, not a local church pastor and his speciality was the gospel not the sacraments which make the gospel visible.

Moreover, the second part of verse 17, the evangelism Paul was commissioned to do was not with words of human wisdom. Literally not in 'wisdom of word' lest the cross of Christ be emptied of its power. This phrase expresses a double renunciation which the apostle Paul had made. On the one hand, he renounced the world's wisdom in favour of the cross of Christ. That's what he preached. On the other hand, he renounced the skills of Greek rhetoric, which were so popular in the Ancient Graeco-Roman world. Instead of human rhetoric, he trusted in the power of God the Holy Spirit. And that double renunciation of human philosophy, for content and human rhetoric, for form, is elaborated later. Charles Hodge, in his fine reformed commentary from the middle of the nineteenth century said, 'Paul was neither a philosopher nor a rhetorician after the Grecian school.'

Conclusion

The ambiguity of the church is the thing I am anxious we should take away and maybe you are thinking of your own church back home. We need to come to terms with it in this way. On the one hand biblical Christians are not perfectionists. We don't dream of developing a perfect church on earth. Billy Graham wisely says, 'By all means look for the perfect church and when you find it, join it, but remember when you join it, it ceases to be perfect.' On the other hand biblical Christians are not defeatists, or pessimists. We don't tolerate sin and error in the community as if it didn't matter.

To perfectionists we say, 'You're right to seek the doctrinal and ethical purity of the church, but you're wrong to imagine that you will ever attain perfection in this life. Not until Christ comes will He present His Bride, the church, to Himself — a radiant church without stain, wrinkle or blemish, holy and blameless.' To pessimists and defeatists we say, 'You're right to acknowledge the reality of sin and error in the church. You're right not to close your eyes to it and pretend that it is perfect when it isn't. But you're wrong to tolerate it.' There is a place for discipline in the church and even, in extreme cases, for excommunication. To deny that Jesus is the Son of God made flesh, to deny the incarnation is anti Christ. We cannot have fellowship with antichrists. And to deny or contradict the gospel of the grace of God, Paul says, is anathema. He called down the judgement of God on those who deny the gospel. In these central matters, about the person and the work of Christ, we cannot tolerate error or sin.

So this is the ambiguity of the church. The church *has been* sanctified, but it is still sinful and called to be holy. The church *has been* enriched, but it is still defective, eagerly waiting for the Second Coming of Christ. The church *has been* united, there is only one church of God in Christ, but it is still unnecessarily divided. So, we are living in between times: between Kingdom come and Kingdom coming; between the divine ideal and the human reality; between the already and the not yet. Not until Christ comes will the ideal become a reality and all ambiguity will cease. Hallelujah!

2. Power Through Weakness
1 Corinthians 1:18–2:5

Introduction

Let us consider the five references to power in this passage:

1:17 'lest the cross of Christ be emptied of its power'.

1:18 'the message of the cross to us who are being saved is the power of God'.

1:24 'to those whom God has called Christ is the power of God'.

2:4 'my message and preaching were with a demonstration of the Spirit's power'.

2:5 'so that your faith might rest on God's power'.

And for the sake of completeness we could add:

2 Cor. 4:7 'to show that the all surpassing power is from God'.

2 Cor. 12:9 'so that Christ's power may rest upon me'.

Here you see seven references to power: the power of God, the power of Christ, the power of the cross and the power of the Holy Spirit.

This concentration on power makes an immediate appeal to us at the beginning of the twenty-first century because we live in a society which positively worships power. Indeed, the three major human ambitions, the pursuit of money, fame and influence, are all a concealed drive for power. We see this thirst for power everywhere: in politics and public life; in big business and in industry; in the professions; in primitive societies in which the shaman or witch doctor trades secret power for money.

Unfortunately, we also see it in the church – in top-level ecclesiastical power struggles, in denominational disputes, in some local churches in which the clergy hold the reins of power in their own hands and refuse to share it either with lay people or, still less, with young people. We see it in para-church organizations, which dream of expanding into world empires. And we also see it here in the pulpit, which is a very dangerous place for any child of Adam to occupy. Power is more intoxicating than alcohol and more addictive than drugs. As Lord Acton said, 'Power tends to corrupt and absolute power corrupts absolutely.'

Lord Acton was a nineteenth-century politician, a friend and adviser of Prime Minister Gladstone, and he was very disturbed, in his day, to see democracy being undermined by this lust for power. He was also a Roman Catholic and in 1870, which was the first Vatican council, he opposed the decision of the council to attribute infallibility to the Pope. He saw it as power corrupting the church.

Now, moving from the Roman Catholic scene to the evangelical scene, I want to tell you frankly that I am scared of the contemporary evangelical hunger for power. Even the quest for the power of the Holy Spirit. Be honest, why do we want to receive power? Is it honestly power for witness? Power for holiness? Power for humble service? Or is it really a mask for personal ambition so that we may boost our own ego? Minister to our own self-importance? Extend our influence, to impress, to dominate, to manipulate? The lust for power is a very dangerous thing and even some evangelism can be a disguised form of imperialism. It can build human empires instead of building the Kingdom of God. There is only one imperialism that is Christian and that is a concern for the imperial majesty of our Saviour, the Lord Jesus Christ. All other imperialisms are sinful.

The Bible contains clear warnings about the use and abuse of power. In the Old Testament, Uzziah, king of Judah, 'was greatly helped until he became powerful'. Then his pride led to his downfall. In contrast, in the New Testament, our Lord Jesus Christ is the perfect symbol of the weakness of humility. He said:

> You know that those who are regarded as rulers of the Gentiles lord it over them, and their high officials exercise authority over them. Not so among you. Instead, whoever wants to become great among you must be your servant, and whoever wants to be first must be the slave of all. For even the Son of Man did not come to be served, but to serve, and to give his life as a ransom for many (Mk. 10:42–5).

In other words, Jesus came not to wield power, but to renounce it. Not to be served, but to serve and to give.

At no point does the Christian mind come into more violent collision with the secular mind than in its insistence on the weakness of humility. The wisdom of the world does not greatly value humility. We've drunk in more than we realize of the power of Nietzsche's philosophy. He worshipped power, dreaming of the rise of a ruling Aryan race, that would be tough, masculine, brash and oppressive. He despised Jesus for His weakness. The ideal of Nietzsche was the *Übermensch*, the super man. The ideal of Jesus was the little child. There was no possibility of a compromise between those two images. We have to choose between them. It is necessary to see what we are going to study in the light of the contemporary lust for power. The central theme of the Corinthian correspondence is not power, as I may have seemed to indicate so far, but power through weakness, divine power through human weakness.

The apostle Paul brings together three striking illustrations of this very same principle.

1) Power through weakness in the gospel itself (1:17–25). Because the weakness of the cross is the power of God.
2) Power through weakness in the converts (1:26–31). God has chosen the weak people to shame the strong.
3) Power through weakness in Paul the evangelist (2:1, 5). He

says he came in weakness, looking to the demonstration
of the Spirit's Power (vv. 3, 4).

Thus the gospel, the converts, and the preachers, or if you pre-
fer it, the Evangel, the evangelized and the evangelist, all
exhibit the same fundamental principle: God's divine power
operates best in the arena of human weakness. That's the
theme. God help us to absorb it and to live it out in our lives.

Power through weakness in the gospel itself (1:17–25)

Every communicator has to answer two questions: What have
I got to say? and How am I going to say it? The first is the
message and the second the method. In the first century AD
of Graeco-Roman culture these two questions were readily
answered. The 'what' of communication was philosophy, the
'how' of communication was rhetoric – an elaborate ornamentation of language and style. But Paul immediately
renounced both. He refused to preach the gospel, as we saw
previously in verse 17, in 'wisdom of world'. In the place of
human philosophy he put the cross; in the place of human
rhetoric, the power of the Holy Spirit. And the cross was both
the wisdom of God and the power of God. Paul enlarges on
this position in verses 18–21 and in verses 22 and 25, with the
hammer blows of repetition that are so important in all our
communication, even today.

I am going to take verse 21 only, in the first example,
because it's a beautifully chiselled sentence. In summary it
says that, whereas the non-Christian world failed, through its
own wisdom, to come to know God, it pleased God through
the folly of the gospel, or the kērugma, to save those who
believe. In verses 22–25 Paul elaborates the same thesis,
namely, wisdom through the folly of the cross and power
through the weakness of the cross. To do so he divides the
human race into three sections: Jews, Gentiles or Greeks and
Christians and he pinpoints the essential difference between
them.

Firstly, verse 22, Jews demand miraculous signs. They were expecting a political Messiah who would drive the Roman legions into the Mediterranean Sea and re-establish Israel's lost national sovereignty. So the Jews demanded appropriate evidence from every revolutionary, every messianic pretender. Give us a sign of power to indicate to us that you are able to do what is expected of the Messiah and drive the Roman legions out of the country. That's why the Jews kept asking Jesus, 'What signs do you do that we may believe in you?'

Secondly, the Greeks search for wisdom. Greece had a very long tradition of brilliant philosophy. The Greeks believed in the autonomy of the human mind and they listened eagerly to every new idea, every speculation, as long as it seemed, to them, to be reasonable. So the Jews demanded power and the Greeks were in search of wisdom.

Thirdly, Christian believers, whether Jews or Gentiles, preach Christ crucified (v. 23). Notice the contrasting verbs. The Jews make demands, the Greeks are seeking and searching, but we proclaim Somebody: the Messiah crucified for us on the cross. But a crucified Messiah was a contradiction in terms. If He was going to drive the Roman legions out of the country, how could He be crucified on a cross? The very word Messiah meant power, splendour, majesty, triumph, and victory. The word crucifixion meant weakness, humiliation and defeat and this was the very opposite.

So the message of Christ crucified provoked different reactions. To the Jews He was a stumbling block. They were expecting this military Messiah riding on a warhorse, at the head of an army. Instead they were offered a pathetic, crucified weakling. It was an insult to their national pride. How could God's Messiah end His life under the condemnation of His own people? How could He end His life under the curse of God on the cross? It was impossible. A crucified Messiah was inconceivable. You can't put the two words together, they make nonsense. The cross was an absolute stumbling block to those who worshipped power.

To the Gentiles, Christ crucified was foolishness. Crucifixion, in the ancient Roman world, was not only a painful execution, it was also a public humiliation, reserved for the dregs of society – slaves and criminals. No free man or citizen was ever crucified. It was inconceivable to them that the Son of God should end His life on a cross. Cicero, the great Roman orator, said on one occasion, 'The very name of the cross, the very word of the cross is absent, not only from the bodies of Roman citizens, because they were never crucified, but also from their minds. They would not even think about it, or imagine it. From their eyes they would never watch a crucifixion and from their ears they would never listen to talk about it.' So horrific was the concept of crucifixion to them.

However, to those who are called God's own people (v. 24), irrespective as to whether they were Jews or Gentiles ethnically, Christ crucified is not weakness, but the power of God. It is not foolishness, it is the wisdom of God. 'For the foolishness of God is wiser than human wisdom and the weakness of God is stronger than human strength' (v. 25).

This whole text is embarrassingly relevant to us today. There are no first-century Jews or Greeks who have survived but there many modern equivalents. The cross is still a stumbling block to all those who, like Nietzsche, worship power, who are confident in their own ability to get to heaven under their own steam, confident of themselves. Or at least if they cannot earn their salvation, they are convinced they can contribute to it. William Temple, Archbishop of Canterbury until he died in the forties, said this, 'The only thing of my very own which I contribute to my redemption, is the sin from which I need to be redeemed.' It is a non-contributory gift of God and we have to humble ourselves to receive it as a free gift.

I remember trying to explain this to a fellow undergraduate in Cambridge. He was very smooth and aristocratic and I was trying to humble him and tell him that he could not do anything to earn his own salvation. Suddenly, without warning, he shouted at the top of his voice, 'Horrible, horrible, horrible!' I was quite surprised. I didn't know I had said anything horrible, but I have often thanked God for that experience. It gave me a glimpse into the arrogance of the human heart. Because we worship power, we want to get there ourselves, make our own contribution. But the cross tells us it is impossible. Christ came and died to save us because we cannot save ourselves. So the cross is a stumbling block to the morally proud.

The cross is also foolishness to the intellectually proud. It makes no sense to them. Sir Alfred Ayer, the Oxford philosopher, hated Christianity and lost no opportunity to be rude about the gospel. As one of the pioneers of so-called logical positivism he wrote *Language, Truth and Logic* and he said, 'Of all the historic religions there are good reasons for regarding Christianity as the worst. Why? Because it rests on the allied doctrines of original sin and vicarious atonement which are intellectually contemptible and morally outrageous.' That is our precious gospel: intellectually contemptible, morally outrageous. That's the wisdom of the world.

To God's people the cross is not weakness but power, it's not folly but wisdom. It's the power of God because through it God saves those who cannot save themselves and it's the wisdom of God because through the cross God has solved not only our problem of sin and guilt, but also His own problem. And it is not wrong to speak of a divine problem or a divine dilemma. We cannot avoid doing so, it arises from God's character of Holy Love. God's dilemma: how could He express His holiness in judging and punishing sin without comprising His love for sinners? Or, how could God express His love in forgiving sinners without comprising His justice in the judgement of sin? How could God be at one and the same time a just God and a saviour? And God's answer was and still is the cross. Because on the cross He took our place, bore our sin, died our death and so paid our debt. On the cross, God demonstrated his justice (Rom. 3:25), and his love (Rom. 5:8). And in that double demonstration of love and justice the wisdom of God is displayed. His wisdom in the foolishness of the cross and His power in its weakness.

Power through weakness in the converts (1:26–31)

Paul had been inviting the Corinthians to reflect on the gospel and its weakness and now he invites them to reflect on themselves and their weakness. Consider the situation in Corinth. 'Not many of you were wise by human standards [of education]; not many were influential [in the community]; not many were of noble birth' (vv. 26–28). In other words, wisdom and power were not conspicuous among the Corinthians. Indeed the opposite had been the case. 'God chose the foolish things of the world to shame the wise; God chose the weak things of the world to shame the strong. He chose the lowly things of this world and the despised things – and the things that are not – to nullify the things that are' (v. 27). It's the same theme: wisdom through folly and power through weakness.

What was the purpose of God in this action? Why did God choose the weak and the foolish and the non-entities? He did it so that nobody might boast in His presence. So that it might be clear beyond any doubt that the credit for their salvation belonged to God and to God alone (vv. 29–32). They couldn't strut round heaven like peacocks displaying their plumage to show they had got there under their own steam. No! God chose the weak and the foolish to demonstrate that no human being may boast in His presence. So, verse 30, 'It is because of him', God, that they, the Corinthians, were 'in Christ Jesus'. They hadn't put themselves in Christ Jesus, God had put them in Christ Jesus. In consequence, Christ Jesus has become for us, on the one hand, the wisdom of God, on the other, the power of God – our righteousness which is justification, our holiness which is sanctification and our redemption which is the redemption of our bodies or our glorification. So all three tenses of salvation past, present and future, justification, sanctification and glorification are due to God's sheer grace, to His wisdom and power, displayed in and through the cross. Wonderful! Therefore, verse 31, quoting Jeremiah 9, he says, 'Let him who boasts boast in the Lord.' For all other boasting is excluded.

It's evident, from this paragraph, that most of the Corinthian converts were drawn from the lower ranks of society. Mostly, they belonged neither to the intelligentsia nor to the city's influential leaders, nor to its aristocracy. On the whole, they were uneducated, powerless, socially despised and probably most of them were slaves. The fact that the gospel reached, saved and changed them was a dramatic illustration of this principle of power through weakness. Is Paul saying that God never calls and saves those who are clever or wealthy, influential or socially prominent? It can't mean that. Saul of Tarsus himself was a notable exception. He had a powerful intellect and personality and yet he had been saved. And even in Corinth, Luke tells us, in Acts 18, Crispus was converted and he was the ruler of the synagogue and in Romans 16, we read, 'Greetings from Gaius,' who was wealthy enough to accommodate and give hospitality to the whole church in his house. And then there was Erastus who was the city's director of public works. Both letters imply that some Corinthian Christians were wealthy because Paul appeals to them to give generously to the impoverished church in Judea. We cannot say that God never calls and saves these people The key to the interpretation of these verses is that in verse 26 Paul writes not 'that not *any* of you' but 'that not *many* of you'. Selina the Countess of Huntingdon, the eighteenth-century evangelical aristocrat, a personal friend of John Wesley and George Whitefield, used to say, as she tried to introduce the British upper classes to the gospel, 'I thank God for the letter *m* in the word many.'

What do we conclude from this? Is it wrong to take the gospel to such elitist groups as students and professional people? No. Paul's emphasis is that God's power operates only in the salvation of the weak. And therefore, if the strong hope to be saved, they've got to become weak first. They have got to acknowledge their inability to save themselves. They may be influential in the community, they may have wealth, they may be very clever, but they have got to humble themselves and admit their weakness in this area: they cannot, by anything they do or contribute, save themselves. Otherwise, God's grace will never reach them. As Jesus said, 'The Kingdom of God belongs to children. Therefore if you adults want to get into it you have got to become like a little child, because the only citizens of the Kingdom of God are children and the childlike' (cf. Mt. 17:3–4). Luther understood the same message, 'Only the prisoner shall be free, only the poor shall be rich, only the weak shall be strong, only the humble shall be exalted, only the empty shall be filled and only nothing shall become something.'

Power through weakness in the evangelist (2:1–5)

Not only were the Corinthian converts weak and feeble but the apostle himself was also weak and feeble. As the great Hudson Taylor sometimes said, 'All God's giants have been weak people.' This was in contrast to the false teachers who liked to think of themselves as super apostles. They were nothing of the kind! They were proud, arrogant, conceited and self-confident, boasting of their wisdom, authority and power.

Notice the cultural background to this situation. Rhetoric, which I have already mentioned, was a systematic, academic discipline, taught and practised throughout the Graeco-Roman world. In the first century AD it had become the primary discipline in Roman higher education. In public debates, in the law courts, and at funerals the rhetoric of display and ornamentation was tremendously popular as a form of public entertainment. Dr Donald Carson has written, 'It is difficult for us, at the beginning of the twenty-first century, to appreciate how influential was this allegiance to rhetoric.' Gradually, it became an end in itself – mere ornamentation with a desire to please the crowd, but without any serious content, and without any serious intent. A sophist was an orator who emphasized style over substance and form over content.

That was the situation in Corinth, where the Christians had assimilated the rhetorical culture of their day and were evaluating Paul's speech according to the commonly accepted criteria. But Paul was resolved not to use ornamental rhetoric lest the audience focus on form rather than on content. And in this situation Paul made this double renunciation that I have already mentioned. He said 'not with words of human wisdom' (cf. 2:1), 'not with eloquence of superior wisdom'. In both texts he uses the same vocabulary – *sophia*, wisdom, is human philosophy, *logos*, utterance, is human rhetoric and he renounced the philosophy and the rhetoric of the Greeks. While the Corinthians loved both, Paul rejected both. In place of philosophy: nothing but the cross; in place of rhetoric: 'I came to you in weakness', as J.B. Phillips puts it, 'nervous and rather shaky.' So he relied on the demonstration, the *apodeixis*, which the Holy Spirit gives to words spoken in human weakness.

These words would not be a very accurate description to many of us contemporary evangelists. Weakness is not an obvious characteristic of ours. In theological colleges, homiletics classes – classes in the topic of preaching, aim to inculcate self-confidence in nervous students. If Paul had enrolled in one of our Bible or Theological Colleges today, he would have been regarded as very unpromising material! And since he was supposed to be a mature Christian, we might even have rebuked him and said, 'Paul, you have no business to feel nervous. Don't you know what it is to be filled with the Holy Spirit? You ought to be strong and confident and bold.' But Paul was of a different opinion. He was not afraid to admit that he was afraid. He came to them in weakness and fear and trembling. True, he had this massive intellect and strong personality, but he was physically frail, we have not forgotten his 'thorn in the flesh', and he was emotionally vulnerable. Second-century tradition says that he was unattractive, small and even ugly with a bald head, beetle brows, bandy legs and a hooked nose. His critics said that his bodily presence was weak and his speech contemptible (10:10).

He was nothing much to look at and he was nothing much to listen to and these disabilities would have disqualified him from succeeding in rhetoric, so consequently in his human weakness he relied on the power of God. He called it a demonstration of the Spirit and the power. Commentators seem to think that really means a demonstration *of* the power, or *by* the power of the Holy Spirit, because every Christian conversion demands a power encounter between Christ and the devil, in which the superior power of Jesus Christ is demonstrated. The Holy Spirit takes our words, spoken in human weakness, and carries them home with power to the heart, the mind, the conscience and the will of the hearers, in such a way that they see and believe. This is the *apodeixis* – the demonstration by the Holy Spirit and His power.

Now don't misunderstand, this is not an invitation to suppress our personality or to pretend we feel weak when we don't. It's not an invitation to cultivate a fake frailty or to renounce arguments. Luke tells us, in Acts 18, that the apostle continued to argue in Corinth and in the following cities that he visited. The Holy Spirit brings people to faith in Jesus, not *in spite* of the evidence, but *because* of the evidence when He opens their eyes to attend to it. Argumentation and the work of the Holy Spirit are not mutually incompatible. The Holy Spirit uses the truth of our argumentation to bring people to Christ. And we must not give up that thoughtful kind of proclamation of the gospel, knowing that human beings cannot save souls, whether by their own personality or their rhetoric or any other power beside. Only the power of God can give sight to the blind and life to the dead and He does it through the gospel of Christ crucified, proclaimed in the power of the Spirit.

So the power in every power encounter is in the cross, for content, and in the Holy Spirit, for communication. I don't like speaking about myself, but let me illustrate with an example from my own experience what Paul writes here in his letter. Many years ago, in about 1958, I was leading a mission in the University of Sydney in Australia and on the final Sunday afternoon I lost my voice entirely. I didn't know what to do, but it was decided that I would do my best. Student leaders laid their hands on me and prayed for me along the lines of 2 Corinthians 12. 'Most gladly will I rejoice in my infirmities that the power of Christ may rest upon me.' They prayed that that Scripture might come true and in my weakness the power of Christ might come upon me. I croaked the gospel like a raven and when it came to give the invitation, people immediately rose from the hall of over a thousand, to come forward. I have been back to Australia about ten times since then and every time somebody has said to me, 'Do you remember that meeting in the Great Hall of the University? I was converted that night.' I have learnt too that it is in our human weakness that the power of God is demonstrated.

Summary

The central theme of the Corinthian correspondence is power through weakness. We have a weak message – the cross, proclaimed by weak preachers, full of fear and trembling and received by weak hearers – the socially despised. But through that triple weakness the power of God was and still is displayed.

Conclusion

Remember in the Judaean desert the devil offered Jesus power and He declined the offer? Instead, He gave Himself voluntarily to that ultimate weakness and humiliation of the cross. In Revelation 4–7, when the door is opened in heaven, the first thing John's eye lit upon was a throne, symbol of power. Sharing the throne with God the Father was a Lamb, as He had been slain: the symbol of weakness on a throne of power. In other words, power through weakness dramatized in God on the cross or in the Lamb on the throne lies at the very heart of ultimate reality and even at the being of God Himself. We pray for one another that this mind might be in us which is and was in Christ Jesus. The Christian leaders, who are needed in the church today, are those who have seen the Lamb on the throne, and who follow the Lamb wherever He goes, knowing that power is best displayed in weakness.

3. The Holy Spirit and Holy Scripture
1 Corinthians 2:6–16

Introduction

You will notice that there is a heavy emphasis in this passage on the ministry of the Holy Spirit where He is mentioned by name, either directly or indirectly, nine or ten times. In particular, the emphasis is on His teaching role as the Spirit of Truth. This is one of the most important New Testament passages in regard to the relation between the Spirit and the Word. We all know that Holy Scripture and Holy Spirit are supposed to have something to do with one another, because the Holy Scripture is the creative product of the Holy Spirit. We say, if we recite the Nicene Creed, that He spoke through the prophets. And we read that 'holy men spoke from God as they were moved [or carried along] by the Holy Spirit' (1 Pet. 1:21). We are going to investigate the precise relationship between the Spirit and the Word in this passage and the part played by the Holy Spirit in the composition of Scripture. Because we evangelical people acknowledge as one of our main distinctives our submission to the supreme authority of Scripture, this is a very important topic.

Before we come to the details, we need first to see the text in its context – a wise hermeneutic principle whenever we are studying Scripture. Everybody agrees that in chapter 2 verse 6 the apostle Paul's argument changes course. Up to this point, he has been emphasizing the foolishness of the gospel. But now, he says, 'We do, however, speak a message of wisdom among the mature.' Paul is not contradicting himself. To quote Professor F.F. Bruce in his commentary on 1 Corinthians, 'The wisdom Paul now says he proclaims is not something additional to the saving message of Christ crucified, it is in Christ crucified that the wisdom of God is embodied. It consists rather, in the more detailed unfolding of the divine purpose summed up in Christ crucified.' But although he says 'we do speak wisdom', he immediately adds three qualifications to be sure that he is not misunderstood:

a) It is wisdom for the mature.

The *teleiōs* is the Greek word. It's not for the unregenerate, it's not even for babes in Christ. Since it is solid food and not milk, it cannot easily be digested. It is for mature Christians who are anxious to penetrate into the fullness of the saving purpose of God.

b) It is wisdom from God.

It's not the wisdom of this age, it's not human philosophy, it's not the wisdom of the rulers of this age, it's not the wisdom of the world. Beginning in verse 7, it is wisdom from God.

c) It is wisdom designed for our glory.

Doxa is the word used and it is essentially an eschatological word referring to our glorification at the end of time and in eternity, when Christ comes in sheer magnificence and we share in His glory and even our bodies are glorified. So the wisdom of God, for the mature, is not just good news of our justification, it is good news of glorification; it alludes to our final perfection as we share in the glory of God.

All this seems to mean that there is a legitimate difference between our evangelistic message on the one hand and Christian nurture on the other. In evangelism we proclaim the folly of the cross which is the wisdom and the power of God. We resolve to know nothing but Jesus Christ and Him crucified. And through this folly of the preached message, the *kērugma* or the gospel, God saves those who believe –

that's evangelism and Christ crucified is at the very forefront of our evangelistic message. In Christian nurture, however, as we build people up into maturity, we want them to understand God's total purpose and especially our forthcoming glorification.

This, verse 7, is God's secret wisdom and it can be known only by revelation. Paul insists in verse 9, a rather loose quotation from Isaiah 64:4, God's wisdom is something which no human eye has seen — it's invisible; no human ear has heard — it's inaudible; and no human mind has ever imagined — it's inconceivable. It's altogether beyond the reach of our eyes, our ears and our minds. It cannot be grasped either by scientific investigation or by poetic imagination. It is absolutely unobtainable by our little finite, fallen and fallible minds. Therefore, if it is ever to be known, only God can reveal it, which is exactly what He has done, verse 10. Many people stop at verse 9, but you must always go on to verse 10. These things that cannot be known by the eye, the ear or the mind, God has revealed by His Spirit.

Let's think, for a moment, about the necessity of revelation. When the apostle says that not even human minds have understood it, he is not denigrating the human mind; he is simply saying that the human mind, capable as it is of remarkable achievement in the realm of the empirical sciences, when it is seeking God, it flounders helplessly out of its depth. And the Old Testament equivalent of verses 9 and 10 is surely Isaiah 55:8–9, where it says, ' "For my thoughts are not your thoughts, neither are your ways my ways," declares the Lord. "As the heavens are higher than the earth, so are my ways higher than your ways and my thoughts than your thoughts." ' Heaven being higher than the earth means infinity. And there is no ladder by which we can climb up into the infinite mind of God. If this little mind cannot fathom the infinite mind of God, how can we know His mind? Answer: we cannot if He remains silent. We could never even begin to know the thoughts of God and the mind of God unless He had spoken. Why, we cannot even read each other's minds, if we are silent, so how much less can we read the mind of God. But God has spoken. You know what is going on in my mind at this moment because I am speaking to you, I am communicating the thoughts of my mind by the words of my mouth. That is exactly what God has done: communicated the secret thoughts in His mind by the words of His mouth. He has spoken. That's how we know what He is thinking.

'God has revealed His thoughts to us by His Spirit' (v. 10). 'Us' is emphatic in the Greek sentence and it must surely refer not to all of us. We are not all direct recipients of a revelation of God. It must refer to the apostles who were the recipients of divine revelation, not only Paul himself, but by extension, his fellow apostles as well. I am reminded of Ephesians 3:5 where we read that the mystery of Christ, the truth about Christ, into which Jews and Gentiles can enter on the same terms, has now been revealed by the Spirit to God's holy apostles and prophets who are the foundation on which the church has been built (cf. Eph. 3:5; 2:20). So this is the context and now in what follows, Paul gives a comprehensive statement of the Holy Spirit's work as the agent of divine revelation which he presents to us in four stages.

1) The searching Spirit (2:10, 11)

Notice that this verb, *searching*, shows quite clearly that the Holy Spirit is personal. You can't search and research unless you have got a mind, and if you have got a mind, you must be a person. Every research worker knows that it's part of their personality that they are searching for the truth. Computers analyse the data fed into them, but true research work requires original investigation and reflection. Because the Holy Spirit is a person, searching the deep things of God, we must never refer to Him as 'it'. He is a *He*, as Jesus made clear in His own teaching. Because He is a person He has a mind of His own with which He is able to think.

Now Paul develops two fascinating pictures to indicate the Holy Spirit's unique qualifications in the work of divine revelation.

a) He searches the depths of God (v. 10)

The verb used there, which means 'to investigate', is the very same word that Jesus has used, or the Greek translation of Jesus' Aramaic, when He applied it to the Jews who *searched* the Scriptures (cf. Jn. 5:39). It refers to diligent study and investigation. Moulton and Milligan, in their famous lexicon, *The Vocabulary of the Greek New Testament*, quoted third-century AD papyrus in which the *searchers*, using the same word, are customs officials who rummage about in our baggage whether we want them to or not. Further, the 'deep things', the Greek word there, became in the second century AD a favourite term used by the Gnostic heretics, who claimed to have been initiated into the deep things of God. It is just possible that in the middle of the first century, Paul deliberately borrowed from the Gnostic vocabulary, insisting here that the deep things of God were known and investigated, not by the Gnostics who claimed to have been initiated into the deep things of God, but by the Holy Spirit alone. Only the Holy Spirit can investigate the deep things of God. So the Holy Spirit is depicted as a restlessly inquisitive research worker, even a deep-sea diver who is seeking to fathom the deepest depths of the infinite being of Almighty God. The Holy Spirit is God exploring the infinity of God.

b) He knows the thoughts of God (v. 11)

'Who among men knows the thoughts of a man except the man's spirit within him?' In the same way nobody knows the thoughts of God except the Spirit of God Himself. Now the thoughts there, are literally the *things* of a man or the *things* of God, maybe the things of a man, mean what we would call humanness – what it means to be a human being. So nobody understands what humanness means except human beings. An ant cannot possibly understand what it means to be a human being, nor a rabbit, a frog, or even a chimpanzee, for all the richness of the DNA that it apparently possesses. Nor even can one human being fully understand another human being. How often, especially as an adolescent, we complained, 'Nobody understands me!' It's true nobody does, in fullness – we don't even fully understand ourselves. Yet to some degree we human beings are self-conscious and self-aware and have some understanding of what humanness means. This is the concept of human self-awareness and self-consciousness that Paul applies to the Holy Spirit. 'In the same way nobody knows the things of God except the Spirit of God' (v. 11b). So the Holy Spirit seems to be likened to the divine self-consciousness or the divine self-understanding. Just as nobody can understand a human being, except that human being himself, so nobody can understand God, except God Himself. Only God knows God. It's reasonable because of His infinity.

To sum up this first truth about the Holy Spirit: the Holy Spirit searches the depths of God, and the Holy Spirit knows the things of God. Both statements indicate that the Holy Spirit has a unique understanding of God because He is Himself God. The question then is what has the Holy Spirit done with what He has searched out and come to know? Answer: He has done what only He is competent to do, He has revealed it. Only He knows God, so only He can make Him known. It's logical. The *searching* Spirit became:

2) The revealing Spirit (2:12)

What the Holy Spirit had searched out and come to know He went on to make known. This has already been stated in verse 10: God has revealed it to us, the apostles, by His Spirit. Let's look carefully at verse 12 where the apostle Paul enlarges on this. 'We', the same emphatic plural of apostolic authority, 'We have not received the spirit of the world, but the Spirit who is from God' – the searching Spirit, the knowing Spirit. And we have received the Holy Spirit in order 'that we might understand what God has freely given to us'. That indicates clearly that God had given the apostles not one, but two separate, related gifts.

Firstly, they received God's salvation, what God has freely given to us. What has He freely given to us? Eternal life – salvation. And *secondly*, He's given us God's Spirit to enable the apostles to understand that salvation. The apostle Paul himself is the best example of having received this double gift of God. First the gift of salvation, then the gift of the Spirit to understand the gift of salvation.

Paul's letters give us a superb exposition of the gospel of grace. How God set His love upon the very people who didn't deserve it. How He sent His Son to die for sinners like us who didn't deserve it. How God raised Him from the dead to demonstrate that He had not died in vain. And how we, by faith inwardly, by baptism outwardly, may become united to Christ in His death and resurrection. It's a moving exposition, which stretches the mind and sets the heart on fire. Where on earth did the apostle Paul get all this wonderful doctrine from? How did he understand all this? How could he make such a comprehensive statement of salvation? Answer: because he had himself received salvation, and because he received the Holy Spirit to interpret his experience to him. Thus the searching Spirit became the revealing Spirit, making God known to the biblical authors, which became:

3) The inspiring Spirit (2:13a)

'This is what we speak…' (NIV), or 'we impart this…' (RSV). This understanding of salvation, which the Holy Spirit had given to the apostles, is now imparted. The searching Spirit, who had revealed God's plan of salvation *to* the apostles, went on to communicate *through* the apostles what they had received. Just as the Spirit did not keep His researches to Himself but revealed them to the apostles, so the apostles, in their turn, did not keep His revelation to themselves but communicated it to others in the New Testament. They knew that they were trustees of the revelation of God. They couldn't claim a monopoly on this divine revelation and keep it to themselves. Truth is for sharing. So they delivered to others what they had themselves received.

Next question: How did they impart the truth that had been revealed to them? Answer: verse 13, 'Not in words taught us by human wisdom but in words taught by the

Spirit'. The same Holy Spirit, who searched the depths of God and who revealed God's secrets to the apostles, now gave the apostles the words with which to communicate them to others. Verse 13 is an unambiguous claim, on the part of the apostle Paul, to what we call 'verbal inspiration' – the inspiration of God extended to the very words which the apostles used in their communication. Those words had been given to them by the Holy Spirit. Now verbal inspiration is a very unpopular doctrine in the church today. And I strongly suspect that is because it is misunderstood and that what people reject is not the true meaning of verbal inspiration but something of their own creation.

Because this is so important I take the liberty of allowing myself a little digression, in order to try to explain what verbal inspiration means. I want to use three negatives about what it does *not* mean and one positive about what it *does* mean.

a) Verbal inspiration does *not* mean that every word of the Bible is *literally* (I emphasize that adverb) true. That's a dictionary definition of verbal inspiration. The true understanding of verbal inspiration does not mean that. No. The biblical authors used a number of different types of literature: history, poetry, proverbs, letters, an apocalypse and so on. There are about twenty different kinds of literature and not all of them are to be interpreted literally. Each is to be interpreted according to its own literary style. We interpret history as history, prophecy as prophecy, poetry as poetry and so on. So what is inspired is the natural sense of the word, according to the intention of each biblical author, whether it is literal or figurative. Some of the Bible is deliberately figurative. For example, 'The heavens declare the glory of God, the firmament shows his handiwork and in them [in the heavens] God has set a tabernacle [a tent], for the sun to live in. And it emerges like a bridegroom out of his chamber and runs like an athlete across the track of the heavens' (cf. Ps. 19). Within three verses the sun is likened to a tent dweller, an athlete, and a bridegroom. You are not going to interpret those literally, are you? Beware of biblical literalism when the biblical authors themselves are not intending you to interpret it literally.

Remember, Jesus Himself was an opponent of biblical literalism when He was speaking symbolically. He said to Nicodemus, 'You have got to be born again.' 'What?' said Nicodemus. 'Re-enter my mother's womb and be born?' 'Don't be such a biblical literalist,' Jesus said. (I am allowing myself a little freedom!) 'I am not talking about a second physical birth.' And then to the woman of Samaria He said, 'If you knew who it is that asks you for a drink, you would have asked of him and he would have given you living water.' 'But you haven't got a bucket,' she replied. He said to her, 'Don't be a biblical literalist. I am speaking of eternal life – symbolically, figuratively.' So we need to understand what type of literature it is. Verbal inspiration does not mean that every word is literally true.

b) Verbal inspiration does *not* mean verbal *dictation*. The Christian understanding of the Bible is very different from the Muslim's understanding of the Koran. Muslims believe that Allah, through the angel Gabriel, dictated the Koran to Mohammed, in Arabic, and that Mohammed had nothing to do but take down the dictation. Christians do *not* believe that about the biblical authors. On the contrary, we believe the biblical authors were persons in full possession of their human faculties. They were not dictating machines, even during the process of inspiration, taking down divine dictation. Thus every biblical author has his own literary style, his own theological emphasis, and these distinctives of each author are not ironed out or destroyed by the process of inspiration. Moreover, many biblical authors were historians. Have you thought how much of the Bible is history? Genesis, Exodus, Leviticus, Numbers, Deuteronomy, Joshua, Judges, Ruth, two books of Samuel, two books of Kings, two books of Chronicles: it's all history. Matthew, Mark, Luke, John, Acts: it's all history. We don't imagine that that history was all supernaturally revealed. No, they did their own historical researches. Luke tells us so. In Luke 1:1–4 he says he had diligently investigated the things that had taken part from the beginning. So divine inspiration and historical research were not incompatible with one another. It's important to remember that. Verbal inspiration does not mean verbal dictation.

c) Verbal inspiration does *not* mean that every text of Scripture is true even in isolation from its *context*. As the Lausanne Covenant said, 'The Bible is without error in all that it affirms.' But not everything included in Scripture is affirmed by Scripture and the best example is seen in the long and tedious speeches of the so-called comforters of Job. You cannot take anything out of the speeches of Job's comforters and declare it to be the Word of God, because they said that Job was being punished for his sins. But Job chapters 1 and 2 affirm that he was not a sinner, he was a righteous man. He feared God and avoided evil and when you come to chapter 42, the last chapter, God says that Job's comforters 'have not said about Me what is right'. God Himself contradicts Job's comforters. So some of what the comforters said is included, not in order to be endorsed, but in order to be repudiated. Now don't misunderstand me, the book of Job *is* the infallible Word of God *if* you take it as a whole if you allow it to interpret itself, but each text is not the Word of God apart from its context.

d) To be positive, verbal inspiration means that what the Holy Spirit spoke through the biblical authors, understood according to its literary genre, understood according to the plain, natural meaning of the words used, understood according to its particular context and the intention of its authors – that is true and without error. There is no need to be ashamed or afraid of verbal inspiration if it is properly understood. It is eminently reasonable because words matter. They are the building blocks of sentences and it is impossible to convey a precise message if you do not choose precise words. I have prepared my lecture because I don't want to confuse you. I have a precise message to convey so I have chosen precise words in which to convey it. Words matter and if they matter to God they matter to us, and vice versa. In the nineteenth century

Charles Kingsley wrote this, 'These glorious things, words, are man's right alone; without words we shouldn't know any more of each other's hearts and thoughts than the dog knows of its fellow dog.' We always think in words and without words all our thoughts would be mere blind longings, feelings which we could not understand ourselves.

So this is the apostolic claim: the same Holy Spirit who searches the depths of God and knows the things of God, who revealed His findings to the apostles, went on to communicate them to others through the apostles in words which He gave them. Thank God for that! He spoke His Word through their words in such a way that their words were simultaneously His words. This is the double authorship of Scripture: God spoke, as the author, through human authors; His words were their words at the same time. This is the meaning of inspiration.

4) The enlightening Spirit (2:13–16)

How are we now to think of those who received this and other letters from the apostle Paul and read them? Were they left to understand by themselves what had been written? Indeed not. The same Holy Spirit who was active in the apostles, who wrote the letters, is active in those who receive and read them. The Holy Spirit was working at both ends of the communicating process, inspiring the apostles and not inspiring us. We are not inspired when we preach and teach, but He illuminates our minds to understand the inspired Word of God. This is implied at the end of verse 13 which the NIV translates, 'expressing spiritual truths in spiritual words'. It's a complicated and rather enigmatic phrase and different English versions explain it in different ways. But I am assuming that the verb *sugkrino*, which can mean 'to combine', means here, as it usually does in the Septuagint (the Greek version of the Old Testament), 'to explain'. I think the RSV is right to translate it, 'interpreting spiritual truths to those who possess the Spirit'.

In other words, the possession of the Holy Spirit is not limited to the biblical authors, He is shared by the Bible readers. Certainly I say again, the Holy Spirit's work of inspiration was unique to the prophets and apostles who were the biblical authors and we preachers must not claim to be inspired, as they were inspired. But to this inspiration of the biblical authors, the Holy Spirit added His work of illumination or interpretation.

Let's distinguish between these words. *Revelation* and *inspiration* are objective. They describe an objective process by which the Holy Spirit drew aside the veil, to reveal Christ and the biblical witness to Christ. *Illumination* is a subjective process by which the Holy Spirit enlightens our minds to understand the revelation that He has given us in Christ and in Scripture. Let me illustrate. Supposing you brought a friend, who is blindfolded, to the unveiling ceremony of a portrait. You have a veiled picture and blindfold eyes. Two processes are necessary before you can read what is written on the inscription under the portrait. First the portrait has to be unveiled. But your friend still can't read it because of the blindfold over his eyes. So the second process is to remove the blindfold so that he can read. For us, there has been an unveiling, which is revelation and inspiration, and an enlightenment, which is the work of the Holy Spirit today.

But what difference does it make? Verses 14 and 15 elaborate this truth and are in stark contrast to one another. Verse 14 begins with a reference to the *psuchikos*, the person without the Holy Spirit, the unregenerate, the natural man (AV). Verse 15 is about the *pneumatikos*, the Christian with the Spirit, the born-again believer. This person with the Spirit discerns or evaluates all things. He has not become omniscient, or infallible, but the things to which he was before spiritually blind, now begin to make sense to him. He understands what he did not understand before, even though he himself is not understood and is discerned by nobody. These details are a little bit difficult, but we understand this: the Christian remains something of an enigma to other people because of the inner secret of his spiritual life which they have not experienced or understood.

I want to ask again, what difference does it make whether you are born again or unregenerate? The answer is that it makes all the difference in the world. It is the indwelling of the Spirit who enlightens our minds to grow in our understanding of the Word of God. And this illumination of our minds, by the Spirit, is a common Christian experience. I can bear witness to it. I used to read the Bible, as a teenager, because my mother had taught my sisters and me to do so. And I continued to do so out of respect for her, but it was all double Dutch to me, I had no idea what it meant. When I came to Christ and was born again, I am not saying that everything was clear, it isn't today, but immediately it began to make sense in a way that it had never done before. William Grimshaw, the eighteenth-century evangelical leader, said after his conversion, 'If God had drawn up His Bible to heaven and sent me down another one it could not have been newer to me than it was.' The Bible becomes a new book, a light unto our path.

Let me digress, because I think there will be in your minds this question: 'If the Holy Spirit is the enlightening Spirit, if He is the illumining Spirit, why don't we agree with one another more than we do? Why do we still disagree? If He enlightens you and He enlightens me, ought we not to agree more than we do?' Well, my general answer is this: we *do* agree with one another a great deal more than we disagree, otherwise we wouldn't be at Keswick. We are all 'one in Christ Jesus' and I would suspect that if we compared notes we would probably agree in 90 to 95 per cent of what we believe. I think we would agree even more with one another if we fulfilled the following conditions:

1) We must accept the supreme authority of Scripture. The big and painful divisions in the church are between the reformed and the un-reformed churches, between those determined to submit to Scripture and those who are unwilling to do so.
2) We must remember that the chief purpose of Scripture is to bear witness to Christ as Saviour. So that in the central truths of the Bible about Christ and salvation by grace alone through faith alone, Scripture is perspicuous – it's

plain, it's transparent, you can see through it. It's in secondary matters that we allow ourselves some liberty for the interpretation.

3) We must develop sound principles of biblical interpretation. It is often said, 'You can make Scripture teach anything you like,' and I agree. You can make Scripture mean anything if you are unscrupulous enough. But if you are scrupulous in the proper use of interpretation, far from you manipulating Scripture, you'll find that Scripture controls you.

4) We have to study Scripture together and not only by ourselves. The church is the hermeneutical community, within which God means His Word to be interpreted. And it's very good not only to read Scripture on our own but to read it in a Bible study group, so that we can help each other, especially if our group is multicultural, to see through each other's eyes things to which we ourselves have been blind. And that's what Paul meant in Ephesians 3:18, 'that we may ... together with all the saints ...[not by ourselves in isolation] grasp...' the full dimensions of His love. We need each other.

5) We must come to the biblical text with a humble, open and receptive spirit, ready for God to break through our cultural defences and to challenge and change us. If we come with a closed mind, then we shall never hear the thunderclap of the Word of God, all we shall hear is the soothing echoes of our own cultural prejudice. We shall see what we want to see, unless we cry to God to open eyes, not just to behold wonderful things in His law. He might say, 'What makes you think I have wonderful things to say to you? I actually have some rather disturbing things. Are you prepared to listen?' 'Oh no!' we say. 'I come to the Bible to be comforted, I don't come to the Bible to be disturbed.' And so we go on in our prejudices because we are not willing to learn. But if we come to Scripture with an open, unprejudiced, humble, receptive mind there is no knowing what God may show us. He continues His work of illumination today.

Conclusion

I end with a little illustration from Charles Simeon, for 54 years the vicar of Holy Trinity in Cambridge at the beginning of the last century, who said, 'If you go out into the garden on a cloudy day when the sun is not shining, and you look at the sundial, all you see is figures but no message. But if the sun breaks through the clouds and shines on the sundial, immediately the finger points.' If I come to Scripture on a cloudy day, with sin between me and God, I will not receive any message from the Word of God; it is just ink and paper. But if the sunlight of the Holy Spirit breaks through on the printed page of my darkened mind and God says, 'Let there be light,' then the finger points and I receive a message that I would never have received otherwise. So the Word and the Spirit belong together. No word without the Spirit, and the Spirit's sword is the Word of God. Let's never separate what God has united in Spirit and Word.

4. The Trinity and the Church
1 Corinthians 3

Introduction

At the beginning of this chapter the apostle refers to the divisions, *schismata*, of the Corinthian Christian community and as he does so, he attributes these divisions not only to sins like jealousy and quarrelling but also to their fundamentally defective understanding of the church. His thesis can be simply stated: if they had a true view of the church, they would have a true view of church leaders. Indeed, if they had a higher view of the church, they would have a lower, more modest view of the leadership and there would be no boasting about men.

Corinthians 3 is one of the greatest New Testament chapters on the church. We evangelicals are often justly criticized for being rugged individualists and for having a poor doctrine of the church. In so far as we do have a poor doctrine of the church, we have departed from the New Testament which has a high view of the Christian community as a community unlike any other community throughout the world and history. So may God give us a balanced, modest and biblical view and understanding of the church.

The connecting link between chapter 2 and chapter 3 is obvious. In chapter 2:14 Paul had insisted that spiritual truths can be discerned only by spiritual people and now he tells the Corinthians, quite bluntly, that they do not qualify as spiritual people – they are unspiritual. 'Brothers, I could not address you as spiritual people,' *pneumatikoi*, 'but as worldly' (v. 1). That's the NIV interpretation, which I think it is an unfortunate translation because Paul's reference is not to the world, *cosmos*, but to the flesh, *sarx*, and the flesh is of course our fallen, self-centred, self-indulgent nature. And in calling them fleshly, *sarkinoi*, or *sarkikoi* (both words are used in different texts), he is not suggesting that they are unconverted. He doesn't call them natural, *psuchikoi*, the word he used in chapter 2:14 for those who don't possess the Holy Spirit. No, they have the Spirit, he addresses them as sisters and brothers, but on the other hand, they are not truly spiritual Christians, governed and controlled by the Holy Spirit. So the apostle uses this term, *sarkinoi*, or *sarkikoi*, developing the same antithesis with which we are familiar from Romans 8 and Galatians 5, between those who live according to the Spirit and those who live according to the flesh – their self-centred, self-indulgent fallen human nature.

Paul has a second way of saying the same thing at the end of verse 1. He describes the Christians not only as carnal or fleshly but as mere babies in Christ. They have been regenerated by the Spirit but they are still infants, *nēpios* in Christ. They had not yet become *teleios*, mature, the word he used in chapter 2:6. Don Carson says that they were 'wretchedly, unacceptably, spiritually immature'. That is their position and I fear that Paul would say the same thing to many Christian congregations throughout the world today. We rejoice in the statistics of church growth evident in many parts of the world. But we don't always remember that it is often growth without depth. There is superficiality and immaturity everywhere in the Christian community today. By what criteria did the apostle conclude the Corinthians were carnal not spiritual, that they were babies and not mature? You can tell a child's age in two main ways: diet and behaviour.

a) Diet

'I gave you milk, not solid food, for you were not yet ready for it. Indeed you are still not ready' (v. 2). Just as babies begin with milk that is easily digestible and only gradually go on to solid food, so Paul had been obliged to feed the Corinthians with spiritual milk – the rudiments of the faith, because they were not yet ready for the meat of the Word of God. In spite of their knowledge (you remember from chapter 1 they had been endowed with knowledge) and the fact that they had been enriched with many spiritual gifts, they were still at an elementary stage in their Christian life. As C.K. Barrett writes in his commentary, 'That was a hard saying for the Corinthians.' They were very pleased with themselves, very complacent. 'But,' the apostle says, 'you are babies. You haven't yet grown up.' What is the difference between meat and milk? Paul is certainly not saying that the cross is rudimentary teaching which Christians later grow out of; we never graduate from the school called Calvary. C.H. Hodge writes, 'The difference between milk and strong meat is simply the difference between the more or less perfect development of the things that are taught.' Gordon Fee says, 'The argument implies that for Paul the gospel of the crucified One is both milk and solid food. As milk it is the elementary good news of salvation. As solid food it is understanding that the entire Christian life is predicated on the same reality of the cross.' I think it is important for us to understand that. We don't grow out of the cross. We grow deeper into the cross and the fullness of its implications. So the continuing need for milk is the first evidence that the Corinthians were babies in Christ, were carnal rather than spiritual. The second criterion by which Christian maturity can be evaluated is:

b) Behaviour (v. 3)

'Since there is jealousy and quarrelling among you, are you not worldly?' or literally, are you not fleshly, carnal? The answer is, of course, yes, because both jealousy and quarrelling are found among the works of the flesh in Galatians 5 – the works of our lower, fallen, self-centred, self-indulgent nature. Then Paul adds, 'If you are quarrelling and are jealous of one another, are you not mere men?' That is to say you are behaving *kata anthrōpon*, according to a human being, following human instead of divine standards. 'For when one says, "I follow Paul," and another, "I follow Apollos," are you not mere men?' Are you not human rather than godly in your outlook? Now I wonder if you've ever noticed Paul's threefold indictment of the Corinthian Christians.

1) Their behaviour was carnal and not spiritual. They were controlled by their selfish nature instead of the Holy Spirit.
2) It was babyish and not mature. They were suffering from what Freud would have called 'infantile regression' – going back to their babyhood having never grown up.
3) They were human and not divine. Their mindset was not godly but ungodly.

Those are three very serious allegations of the Corinthian community and the evidence for their carnality, immaturity and ungodliness was partly their doctrinal diet – still learning the A B C, and partly their moral failures – their jealousy and their quarrelling.

I hope that all of us are really concerned that the church, our church, will grow into maturity. Because I think there are many church leaders here, I venture to digress a moment and ask if you are very familiar with Colossians 1:28–29? I believe that those two verses are a great motto for any minister or church leader to have. This is what the apostle writes: 'We proclaim Christ, warning everybody and teaching everybody in all wisdom in order that we may present everybody mature in Christ.' That was Paul's ambition. Now we think of him as a missionary, a church planter and an evangelist. However, he is not just concerned with the planting of the church, but that it will grow into maturity in Christ. And his desire is that everybody should do so. This is not out of anybody's reach. We proclaim Christ, warning *everybody,* teaching *everybody,* in all wisdom that we may present *everybody* mature in Christ. What a motto to have! What an ambition and a goal to have for the congregation that God has called us to serve.

Now the apostle delves deeper. He argues that the Corinthians have a defective understanding of the church, or they would not behave as they were doing, and he develops three pictures of the church, all of which have important implications.

1) You are God's field (5–9a)

Paul uses an agricultural metaphor. He begins by asking two indignant questions, 'What, after all, is Apollos? And what is Paul?' (v. 5) He doesn't politely ask, '*Who* do you think we are?' He deliberately uses the neuter, '*What* do you think we are that you should pay us such an exaggerated deference?' As Bishop J.B. Lightfoot comments, 'The neuter is much more emphatic than the masculine, it expresses greater disdain.' He is debunking himself and Apollos. We are not masters to whom the Corinthians owed their allegiance, we're only servants, *through* whom you came to believe, not servants *in* whom you came to believe. We are not the objects of your faith; we are not the authors of your faith; we are only instruments through whom God has been at work in order to elicit your faith. And further, this came about as the Lord Jesus has assigned to each his task (v. 5a). So neither the Corinthians nor their leaders had anything to boast about.

In verses 6–8 the apostle identifies the different tasks in the church, illustrating them from his agricultural metaphor – you are God's field – and applying them to himself and Apollos. There are three main tasks to be done if a field is ever to produce a harvest: first, planting the seed, second, watering the seed and third, causing the seed to sprout – sowing, irrigation and growth. So how does Paul apply this to the Corinthian experience? Answer: he applies it chronologically, verse 6, 'I planted the seed,' he said, 'I was the first to come to Corinth.' He came during his second missionary journey about AD 50. He planted the seed, he planted the church. After him came Apollos who watered the seed that the apostle Paul had planted and then he moved on. These two men did their pioneer tasks in relation to the seed, but God made it grow.

The tenses of the verb, in the Greek sentence, enforce this. In verse 6, 'I planted' is an aorist. Paul came to Corinth, did his job, moved on. Then came Apollos who watered the seed and that verb, 'watered', is another aorist. He did what he had to do and then he too moved on, but God made it grow. And that is an imperfect tense, so that all the time when Paul was sowing, and Apollos was watering, God was giving the growth, causing the seed to sprout. So Paul's and Apollos' ministries would not have been of any great value if God had not given growth to the seed.

Now Paul compares the three actors involved, Paul, Apollos and God, with each other. In the evangelization of Corinth and the establishment of the church there, verse 7, neither the planter nor the waterer is anything because both the planting and the watering are unskilled and somewhat mechanical jobs. Anybody can do them, it doesn't require any professional expertise to drop seeds into the soil and water them. What really matters is neither the planting nor the watering, but rather the causing of the seed to sprout and to bear fruit. No human being can do it. Paul couldn't do it with all his apostolic authority; Apollos couldn't do it with all his knowledge of the Scriptures and his famous eloquence. Only God makes things grow.

Now Paul adds a further point, which demonstrates the stupidity of the Corinthians' behaviour. So far he has insisted that the planters and the waterers count for nothing in themselves, so it is silly to exalt their ministries. They have one purpose (8a), and their different tasks of planting and watering serve the same goal, namely, to secure a good harvest, so it's silly to put them in competition with one another. Further, each will be rewarded according to his labour (8b). God will do this on Judgement Day, so it's silly of the Corinthians to anticipate the Day of Judgement by promoting different personalities now. And the conclusion, verse 9, is, 'We are God's fellow workers; you are God's field.' Since the aim of the whole passage is to downplay the role exercised by human leaders, it seems very unlikely that it means we are the privileged workers with God. That is, He is working there and we are working there and we are doing it together. It is much more likely that it means we are fellow workers, that is Paul and Apollos, in the service of God. He is not speaking here of the privilege of working with God, as the Revised English Bible translates it, 'We are fellow workers in God's service.'

What can we learn from this first, agricultural metaphor? The metaphor of the field, the planting, the watering, the giving of the increase does not teach everything about Christian ministry. It's always dangerous to push an analogy beyond the point at which the metaphor is being made or the analogy is being drawn. It's very dangerous to argue from an analogy, that because the church is a field, therefore everything about fields has a parallel in the church. No, we have to ask, at what point is the analogy being made? This says nothing about spiritual gifts or gifts in distinction to roles and offices, or the honour that is attached to being an evangelist or a missionary or a pastor; other passages of the New Testament teach those things – this one doesn't. There is one main point that this is intended to teach: we human workers have very little importance in comparison with God who gives the growth. God allocates the tasks, God gives the growth, God rewards the labourers, so we must not give glory to ourselves, as leaders, or to our fellow workers, but to God alone. The church would be a much happier place and a much more harmonious community if we remembered this elementary principle. We don't matter in comparison to Him.

2) You are God's building (9b–16)

Paul moves on to an architectural metaphor. Whether we are cultivating a field or whether we are erecting a building, we are a team – a team of farmers, a team of builders. We are not labouring on our own. We are serving a common enterprise and we are pursuing a common goal. Just as in God's field one plants and another waters, so in God's building one lays the foundation, another erects the superstructure upon it. However, the two metaphors don't make precisely the same point. The emphasis in God's field is that only God gives the growth and the emphasis in God's building is that only Christ is the foundation. Indeed, Christ crucified.

So once again the apostle Paul applies the metaphor to himself, to Apollos, to other church leaders in Corinth, 'By the grace that God has given to me' (v. 10), a phrase that comes five times in his letters, and always refers to his commissioning as an apostle of Jesus Christ. 'By the grace that God has given to me, I laid a foundation as an expert builder.' The word expert is *sophos*, meaning wise. I am a wise builder. Perhaps he is again saying that the true wisdom is Christ even though he seems to be folly to some people. Certainly Paul has been given the pioneering task of preaching Christ crucified. And he goes on, 'but somebody else is building on the foundation that I laid.' There is no mention of Apollos by name here, because several teachers have followed Paul, both good and bad, both true and false.

His main point is to sound a warning that all of us who are Christian teachers need to heed. It's a warning both about the foundation we lay and about the superstructure we erect upon it. Each one should be careful how he builds. And what carefulness does the apostle have in mind? Well, think first about the foundation. Builders, having laid the foundation, should not tamper with it. They should not try to dig it up or relay it. Because (v. 11) there is only one foundation and nobody can lay any other foundation except the one that is already lying there, which is Jesus Christ. This is the foundation that Paul lays (v. 10). 'The church's one foundation is Jesus Christ her Lord' – the only authentic Jesus Christ there is, not some false Christ, but the Christ of the apostolic witness, Christ crucified and also, of course, risen and reigning. C.K. Barrett writes, 'Paul doesn't mean that it would be impossible to construct a community on a different foundation, but only that such a community would not be the church. The church only exists when it is built upon the one foundation of Jesus Christ.'

We move on to the superstructure. Builders must be very careful about the materials they use in the erection of the superstructure and, broadly speaking, there are only two possibilities. Either gold, silver and costly stones, probably meaning not jewels, but a stone like marble. These are valuable and durable and they represent the true teaching which will stand the test of time and of the Judgement Day. Or, the alternative is cheap, perishable materials like wood, hay and straw, representing false teaching, the wisdom of the world. In both cases (v. 13), the quality of the material used by the builders, that is by the teachers, will be shown for what it is because the Day of Judgement will bring it to light. It will be revealed by fire which will test the quality of every teacher's instruction.

What will be the result of this trial by fire? Answer: just as there are two possible materials, so there are two possible consequences. Either (v. 14) the builder's work will survive because it has been made of durable material – gold, silver, marble – and the builder will receive his reward. Or (v. 15), his work will be consumed because it is made of combustible materials – wood, hay and straw, in this case he will suffer loss. His teaching will not survive, it will be seen to be valueless, and he will lose his reward. But he himself, in the mercy of God, will be saved, although only as one escaping through the flames – or as we might say, 'by the skin of his teeth'. He will not lose his own salvation even if what he has taught will all be burnt up as valueless. There is no allusion here to purgatory; the fire is not a purgatorial fire. The reference in this passage is to teachers, in particular, and not to all believers, who Roman Catholics believe will have to pass through purgatory. The purpose of the fire is not to purify here, as in purgatory, but to test teaching and pass judgement on it.

There is a solemn warning here to all Christian teachers. The Christian teaching ministry is very important. It is designed to build up the church into maturity and we must be sure that our teaching is authentically Christian. If what we teach is true, biblical, balanced, we will be adding gold, silver and marble to the foundation and it will last. But if what we teach is unbiblical, the wisdom of the world, then we are adding a ramshackle superstructure of wood and hay and stubble which will not survive. Thus what we teach may either bless the church or harm it. It may last only for a time or it may last for eternity. So let us be careful if we are Christian teachers. May God enable us to be all the more conscientious in what we teach.

3) You are God's Temple (16–17)

This is an extension of the architectural metaphor because a temple is a building, but it is a special kind of building. And the apostle develops it differently because he is thinking of the Holy of Holies. It is, then, an ecclesiastical or religious metaphor. He begins (v. 16) with, 'Don't you know that you are the temple of God?' Paul asks that question, 'Don't you know?' ten times in 1 Corinthians. He obviously thinks that Christian knowledge is very important. 'Don't you know that your body is the temple of the Holy Spirit?' 'Don't you know that you belong to Christ?' 'Don't you know that the local church is God's sanctuary?' 'Don't you know this?' His implication is this: if you did know it, you would behave differently. Knowledge is in many ways the secret of sanctification. We need to know these things, to take them in and to understand them, to act upon them, and then our behaviour will be different. So Paul attributes the Corinthians' failures to their ignorance or their forgetfulness of some truth.

In the Old Testament the essence of the temple and of the Holy of Holies in Jerusalem, as in the tabernacle before it, was that it was the dwelling place of God. 'I will dwell among them' (Ex. 25:8). And God promised that the shekinah glory, the symbol of His presence, would inhabit and illumine the Holy of Holies. Notice the major promise about the rebuilt temple, ' "And the name of the city will be: THE LORD IS THERE," ' (Ezek. 48:35). It's very clear in the Old Testament.

In the New Testament God's temple or dwelling place is not a building but a people. Now it is the individual Christian's body. 'Don't you know that your body is the temple of the Holy Spirit?' Now it is the local church as here in verse 16 and indirectly in Ephesians 2:22, 'In Christ you are being built together to become a dwelling in which God lives by His Spirit.' So the individual Christian, the local community, the universal community are all said to be the temple in which God dwells. And in His sanctuary today, the church, there is neither an image as there was in pagan temples, nor a symbol, like the shekinah glory, but the Holy Spirit of God Himself, in person. So the sacred wonder of the church is that it is the dwelling place of God by His Spirit.

Of course, as I have said, the church means people and not buildings. God's presence is not tied to buildings. God's presence is tied to His covenant people, His redeemed people whom He has promised never, never, to forsake. So wherever *they* are *He* is also, as in this tent. When we leave the tent we do not leave Him and He does not leave us. He is with His people always, especially in our worship when thousands gather together, there He is through Christ by the Holy Spirit in the very midst of His people. Wonderful!

Because of the sacred nature of the Christian community, as the dwelling place of God, it must not in any way be dishonoured, either divided by jealousy and quarrelling or deceived by false teaching, or defiled by immoral conduct. These are acts of sacrilege which effectively destroy the Christian community as the temple of God and that's why Paul goes on to say, 'If anybody destroys God's temple, God will destroy him' (v. 17), perhaps the most severe saying in the whole of this letter. And surely, the one who destroys the temple cannot be a true believer. He must be, probably, a nominal Christian. He will be destroyed, and I fear that must mean hell, because hell is often referred to as destruction in the New Testament.

We need to keep reminding ourselves that the church is the temple of God. Our local church may be full of unpleasant people we don't like, but when we see these people we need to whisper under our breath, 'You are the temple of the living God. God, through Christ, by His Spirit dwells within you.' And how we should love those who are the temple of God.

You will have noticed Paul's Trinitarian portrait of the church which highlights the role of God, Father, Son and Holy Spirit, in relation to the church. And because it exalts God, Father, Son and Holy Spirit, it downplays the role of human beings. What matters most about the church, as God's field, is that God Himself causes the growth. What matters most about the church, as God's building, is that Jesus Christ is its only foundation. And what matters most about the church, as God's temple, is that it is the dwelling place of the Spirit. This is the apostle's vision of the church: it owes its existence and its growth to God the Father, it's built on the foundation of God the Son and it's indwelt by God the Holy Spirit. It is a unique Trinitarian community. And there is no other community in the world which even remotely resembles it.

In verses 18–23 the apostle wraps up his godly perspective on the church with further reference to wisdom and folly. The wisdom of God includes this new community that he has been writing about, so if the Corinthians belittle God's church by exalting human beings, they are showing their folly and not their wisdom. 'Do not deceive yourselves. If any one of you thinks he is wise by the standards of this age [according to the prevailing wisdom of this age], he should become a fool [in the eyes of the world] so that he may become wise [truly wise that is]. For the wisdom of this world is foolishness in God's sight' (18, 19). And Paul goes on to quote two verses from the wisdom literature of the Old Testament, one from the Psalms, the other from Job, both of which express God's rejection of worldly wisdom.

So what is needed? The Corinthians need to repent of their boastful, self-centred human wisdom. They need to develop a new humility, summed up at the beginning of verse 21, 'no more boasting about men'. That is the climax to the chapter and the verse I want you to take away with you. Paul goes on to finalize his argument. Instead of taking pride in their leaders, and claiming to belong to their leaders, the exact opposite was the case: 'All things are yours, Paul is yours, Apollos is yours, Peter is yours' (v. 21b). In other words, far from belonging to their leaders, saying 'I belong to Paul,' their leaders belong to them. Don't say, 'I belong to Paul, I belong to Apollos,' because Paul and Apollos and Peter are yours – you are not theirs. More than that, not only are their leaders theirs, but all things are theirs, including the world, life, death, the present, the future – 'it's all yours' – an incredible statement. And the reason it is ours is that we belong to Christ and it belongs to Christ. He is the heir of all things and we are in Him, so we are fellow-heirs with Christ, and everything that He will inherit, we will inherit.

This question of who belongs to whom in the Christian community is still vital today. When I was ordained as a deacon in the Church of England, more that fifty years ago, you were taught, when writing to your bishop, to begin, 'My lord', or 'My lord Bishop', and to end, 'I am your lordship's obedient servant'. I gave it up after the first few letters, because I reckoned if anybody was anybody's obedient servant, he was mine!

Along the same lines, I doubt if pastors are wise if they ever use the possessive adjective in relation to the church, referring to 'my church', 'my congregation', 'my people', because they don't belong to us. We have no proprietary rights over them. It would be entirely biblical for them to refer to us as 'their minister', 'their pastor', but we should not refer to them as 'our people'. When we speak of them it would be much more modest to say, 'They are the people whom God has called me to serve and I am their servant, they are not mine.'

Conclusion

We earnestly need to develop a healthy biblical understanding of the church, for only then will we have a healthy understanding of the leadership of the church. We must not define the church in terms of its leaders. We must, rather, define the leaders in relation to the church. We must renounce secular views of the church as if it were a merely human institution, like any other corporate body with human leaders, wielding human authority as 'lionized' celebrities. All that must go. In its place we need to develop a godly view of the church as a unique community unlike any other community, the covenant people of God, the redeemed people of God, in which ministers give humble service and there is no boasting about human beings. For all boasting is directed to God the Holy Trinity, to God the Father who alone gives growth to the seed, to God the Son who alone is the foundation of the church, and to God the Holy Spirit who alone indwells and sanctifies the community. 'No more boasting in men' (v. 21). 'Let him who boasts boast in the Lord' (1:31).

5. Models of Ministry
1 Corinthians 4

Introduction

There is much contemporary confusion today about the nature of the pastoral ministry. What are clergy? If I may use that word. Are they primarily priests, presbyters, pastors, prophets, preachers or psychotherapists? Are they administrators, facilitators, managers, social workers, liturgists or evangelists? There are many options to choose from and this uncertainty is by no means new. Throughout its long history the church has oscillated between two opposite extremes: clericalism and anticlericalism. Clericalism puts clergy on a pedestal and almost worships them; anti-clericalism knocks them off their pedestal and declares them to be redundant. Now that many churches, throughout the world, have recovered the Pauline doctrine of the 'every member' ministry of the body of Christ, radical questions are being asked. Are clergy necessary any longer? Are they not superfluous? Wouldn't the church be healthier without them, so that we all had a ministry? And should we perhaps found a society for the abolition of the clergy? In Mark Twain's *The Adventures of Huckleberry Finn* there is a passage where Huck got into conversation with Joanna, the daughter of Peter Wilks, who had just died. And he said that in the church of the Reverend Harvey Wilks, her uncle in Sheffield, there were no less than seventeen clergy, though he added, 'They don't all of 'em preach the same day, only one of 'em.' 'Well,' says Joanna, 'what does the rest of 'em do?' 'Well nothing much,' says Huck. 'They loll around and pass the plate and one thing or another, but mainly they don't do nothing.' 'Well then,' says Joanna with wide-eyed astonishment, 'what are they for?' 'Why,' he says, 'they are for style, don't you know nothing?'

This confusion goes right back to the very beginning. Think again of this first-century Corinthian church in which different factions claimed the patronage of particular leaders. Paul was absolutely horrified by this personality cult – 'I belong to Paul, I belong to Apollos' – asking, 'What on earth do you think we are?' Now, in chapter 4, he answers his own question, saying, 'This is how one should regard us' (v. 1 RSV). And he proceeds to give four essentials of authentic pastoral leadership. They describe Paul's own, unique apostolic leadership but they also apply to Christian pastoral leadership today. Pastors are:

1) Servants of Christ (1a, 3)

Before they are ministers of the Word, and before they are ministers of the church, they are ministers of Christ. They must have a personal relationship to the Lord Jesus Christ. The word he uses here for ministers is a lowly word. It is well translated by one commentator as, 'We are Christ's underlings.' There are, of course, other New Testament texts that emphasize the nobility of the pastorate. For example, 'If anybody desires to be an overseer, a pastor, he desires a noble task.' It is a noble thing to be a pastor. And Paul calls the church to hold its pastors in high esteem and to love them on account of their own ministry or work. Nevertheless, Paul begins his account of his ministry, not with a title of honour or glory, but with a title of lowliness. The Revised English Bible says, 'We are Christ's subordinates.' Fundamental to all Christian ministry and leadership is a humble, personal relationship with the Lord Jesus Christ Himself. A devotion to Him, expressed in daily prayer, and a love for Him, expressed in daily obedience.

In addition to being Christ's underlings, we are accountable to Him for our ministry, for He is our Lord and He is our Judge. This is both *comforting* and *challenging*. Comforting because it enables us to say, 'I care very little if I am judged by you or by any human court; indeed I do not even judge myself' (v. 3). Verses 4–7 enlarge on this. 'My conscience is clear' (v. 4), literally 'I know nothing against myself.' But even a clear conscience doesn't prove me innocent. It is the Lord Jesus who judges me. 'Therefore judge nothing before the appointed time [premature judgements are always unwise]; wait till the Lord comes' (v. 5). For He is the Judge and we are not judges of one another. As Jesus said in the Sermon on the Mount, 'Judge not that you be not judged' (Mt. 7:1 RSV).

That does not mean that we suspend our critical faculties, but it does mean that we don't stand in judgement on people as if we were their judges, for we are not. When He comes, Jesus will bring to light what is at present hidden in darkness and He will expose even the secret motives of human hearts; nothing is concealed from Him. So there will be no possibility of any miscarriage of justice, even the secrets of our lives are known. And it is then that each of us will receive either praise or maybe censure from Christ.

Now, verse 6, I am applying this principle, he says, to myself and to Apollos for your benefit, so that you may learn from us the meaning of the saying, 'Don't go beyond what is written,' or, as I think it should be better translated, 'Don't go beyond Scripture.' Scripture is what is written and when you are boasting of one leader against another, you are going against Scripture, against what is written. And don't make comparisons either, taking pride in one leader over against another. Comparisons, as we often say, are odious. So, verse 7, he asks a series of questions, 'Who makes you different from anybody else? [All distinctions come from God.] What do you have that you did not receive? And if you did receive it, why do you boast as though you did not?' Boasting is absurd. So the whole passage emphasizes that as ministers of Christ we are accountable to Him for our ministry.

Don't misunderstand this. We must, of course, listen to human criticism, we mustn't just sweep it under the carpet and refuse to listen. It may be painful, particularly if it's untrue, unfair or unkind. But ultimately, even though we listen to human criticism, we never forget that we are accountable to Christ. And the Lord Jesus is a much more merciful judge than any human being, committee, council or synod. So that tells us what to do with anonymous letters. I have received a number in my day. We shouldn't take them too seriously. If somebody doesn't have the courage to announce their identity, we should treat their criticism with a fair degree of cynicism. Do you know the story of Joseph Parker, who was minister of the City Temple at the end of the last century? One day he was climbing up to his pulpit, when a lady in the gallery threw a piece of paper at him. He bent down, picked it up and read it. It had one word on it, 'Fool.' So Joseph Parker began his sermon that day by saying, 'I have received many anonymous letters in my life and previously they have been a text without a signature, but today, for the first time, I have received a signature without a text!' We take human criticism seriously, but anonymous letters not so seriously. It's a very comforting thing to be accountable to God, to Christ and not to any human being or court.

But if, on the one hand, it is a *comforting* thing to be accountable to Him, on the other hand, it is a *challenging* thing – His standards are high and holy. Although much of a pastor's, and a leader's work is unseen and unsupervised by human beings, nevertheless, we are always in His presence. If we remembered this we would never grow slack or careless. If we remember that Jesus Christ is watching us and that one day we will be accountable to Him, then we will, I think, live at the highest possible level in His presence. We are Christ's underlings responsible to Him.

Pastors are not only servants of Christ they are also:

2) Stewards of revelation (1b, 2)

Paul moves from our general responsibility as servants to our more particular responsibility as stewards. Now it is quite true that the Greek word for stewards, *oikonomoi*, is not used in the

Greek text, but the idea is plainly there. The NIV says, 'We are those entrusted with the secret things of God.' The RSV translates it, 'We are stewards of the mysteries of God.' Stewards were dispensers. A steward in a household received food and clothing from the householder and dispensed it to the household. God has given us His revelation and we dispense the revelation, we teach it to others in the church. So God's mysteries, of which we are stewards, are of course His revealed secrets, previously concealed, but now revealed – truths that are known only by revelation, truths about Christ and His salvation and the fact that we are members of the universal Body of Christ, whether we are Jews or Gentiles, on the same terms. This incorporation of Jews and Gentiles in the church is one of the great mysteries that Paul said had been revealed to him. So of these revealed truths, contained in the New Testament now and in the gospel, the apostles were the original stewards: 'God has revealed these things to us apostles, by His Spirit' (2:10). Although this refers, in the first instance, to the apostles, it also applies to Christian pastors and teachers today. God has committed the Scriptures to us in order that we may expound and teach them to others in the church. This reminds us of three things:

1) Pastors are primarily teachers. That is very clear in the New Testament. One of the chief evidences is in 1 Timothy 3, where Paul gives ten or eleven qualifications for the pastorate and nine or ten of them are what you might call moral qualities: not drunk, gentle, not hungry for money, etc. Then he includes what you might call a 'professional quality' – *didaktikos*, having a gift for teaching. A candidate for the pastorate would not need to have a gift for teaching unless the pastorate was a teaching ministry: it is a teaching ministry. And it is plain that nobody should enter it without having some gift for teaching. Pastors are essentially teachers.

2) What we teach has been entrusted to us. We haven't invented it, it's not our own, it has been given to us by God.

3) We are called, above all else, to be faithful to the Scripture

that has been entrusted to us. So the Revised English Bible translates verse 2, 'Now stewards are required to show themselves trustworthy.' It's all a play on words about trust and trustworthiness. We might say that having received a trust and been appointed trustees of the New Testament, we are expected to be trustworthy. But it is very easy to be unfaithful stewards and I am afraid that we have to admit there are many such in the Christian community throughout the world today: rejecting the authority of the Word of God; preferring their own teaching; neglecting to study it; failing to relate it to the real contemporary world; manipulating it to mean what they want it to mean; selecting from it what they like and discarding what they don't like; even contradicting its plain teaching and substituting their own threadbare speculations; flagrantly disobeying its ethical teaching. No wonder the church is languishing in many parts of the world because of these unfaithful stewards who, in different ways, fail in their trusteeship.

Donald Coggan, a preacher himself, was a great believer in the teaching of the Word of God. He wrote three different books on preaching and in one, *Stewards of Grace*, he writes:

> The Christian preacher has a boundary set for him. When he enters the pulpit, he is not an entirely free person. There is a very real sense in which it may be said of him that the Almighty has set him his bounds that he shall not pass. He is not at liberty to invent or choose his message, it has been committed to him and it is for him to declare, expound and commend it to his hearers. It is a great thing to come under the magnificent tyranny of the gospel.

So our boundaries are set for us. We expound Scripture and nothing else. We are servants of Christ and we are stewards of revelation.

And now, prepare yourself for a shock. Pastors are:

3) The scum of the earth (8–13)

The apostle uses three very vivid pictures from the Graeco-Roman world of his day, to illustrate what he is talking about. He takes us into a) the public amphitheatre in which criminals fight with gladiators or wild animals, even to the death; b) a kitchen in which the floor is swept and the cooking vessels are scraped; and c) a plague-ridden city in which scapegoats are sacrificed to the pagan gods. They are three very vivid metaphors and I think we need to spend a little time on each of them.

a) Paul takes us into an amphitheatre on a public holiday (v. 9). Imagine the arena packed with excited crowds. Event follows event throughout the day and at the grand finale, criminals are thrown to the lions or forced to fight with gladiators. One commentator says, 'God has put us apostles last on the programme of the day's sport like criminals condemned to die in the arena.' We have become a spectacle to the whole universe; to angels and humans we are like a bit of cosmic theatre (v. 9b).

Paul is deliberately contrasting himself with the smug security and self-satisfaction of the Corinthian Christians. 'Already,' he says, not without a touch of sarcasm, 'you have all you want! Already you have become rich.' 'Already,' he might have added for the third time, 'you have become kings – and that without us' (v. 8). So twice he uses the 'already' of a realized eschatology. And the third phrase means the same thing, although he does not use the word 'already'. They are enjoying a private little millennium of their own: eating, drinking, feasting, reigning and celebrating. 'Well,' Paul says, 'we wish we could get there with you, and be kings with you, but we know,' he implies, 'the only path to glory is the path of suffering.' It was for Jesus and it is for the followers of Jesus. We are like exhibits in the amphitheatre – condemned to die for Christ. 'You are kings, but we are criminals' is the striking contrast that he makes.

b) When Paul takes us into a kitchen, he uses two very
   unusual Greek words: *perichotharmita* means sweepings or
   rinsings, while *peripseema* means scrapings from a dirty
   saucepan or other kind of pot and both of them, if I may
   quote another commentator, are 'the filth that one gets rid
   of through the sink or the gutter'. Not very polite to us as
   leaders, is it!

   Now he takes us out of the amphitheatre, out of the
   kitchen, and…

c) Into a plague-ridden Greek city stricken by some calam-
   ity. In order to appease the supposed anger of the pagan
   gods, some wretches are taken from the community and
   are thrown into the sea and drowned. These scapegoats
   were called the scum of the earth. And that is what we are,
   says the apostle Paul.

You will agree these are extraordinary statements. And in
verses 10–13 he explains what he is talking about. He is
referring to his sufferings in contrast to Corinthian complacency. He is being ridiculed for Christ. 'We are fools for
Christ' (v. 10), 'but you, you are wise.' Notice the reference
to weakness and strength, wisdom and folly, with which we
began our Bible studies. 'We are weak,' he goes on, 'you are
honoured but we are dishonoured, despised and rejected like
our Master. We are hungry, thirsty, in rags, brutally treated,
homeless, persecuted, slandered. We work with our own
hands, etc. etc. Indeed, we are the scum or the refuse of the
world' (cf. vv. 10–13). As we enjoy the safety and comfort of
the Keswick tent and the grandeur of the lakes and moun-
tains, it all sounds extremely remote from us. In fact, the dif-
ficulty we have in applying words like these to ourselves may
indicate how far we have drifted from the New Testament.
Today, even in our non-Christian society, even in a pluralistic, secular culture, it is still a tolerably respectable thing to be
a pastor. However, it is not always so and it should definitely
not be taken for granted.

I speak very personally now, but I believe that we need
urgently to hear again the words of Jesus: 'Woe unto you
when all men speak well of you.' Beware of the temptation

to be a popular preacher. I doubt very much if it is possible to be popular and faithful at the same time. We either go for popularity at the expense of faithfulness, or we are determined to be faithful at the expense of popularity. We have to choose between them; it is not possible to be both simultaneously. For the cross is still foolishness to some and a stumbling block to others. What is it about the gospel that is so unpopular? Why is it that if we are loyal and faithful in our preaching and teaching we will suffer for it? Why will we be ridiculed? What is it about the gospel that is so offensive? Let me give three answers that may, or may not, be helpful.

1) The gospel offers eternal life as a free gift. 'The wages of sin is death, but the gift of God is eternal life through Jesus Christ' (Rom. 6:23). But we are such proud creatures that we don't want to be given a free gift. We looked at this earlier. We'd do anything to be able to earn our salvation, to achieve it or, at least, contribute to it. We need to remember that eternal life, salvation, is an absolutely free, utterly undeserved and totally non-contributory gift of God. The only thing we contribute is our sin and we find that unbearably humiliating.

2) The gospel not only offers eternal life as a free gift, but it proclaims salvation in Jesus Christ alone and declares that He is the only Saviour. He is unique in His incarnation, in His atonement and in His resurrection. There is no other leader who is the God-Man. There is no other leader, all through history, who has died for the sins of the world. And there is no other leader who has risen from the dead and conquered death. So we are not content to say that Jesus is 'the great'. We can say that Alexander was the great, we can speak of Napoleon the great, Charles the great, but not Jesus the great. He isn't the great, He is the Only, there is nobody like Him. He has no peers, no competitors and no rivals. He is unique. In this pluralistic world, that is anathema. Pluralism and post-modernism means we all have our own truth, but we mustn't try to persuade anybody to accept our truth. There is no such

thing as a universal truth, or a truth that is objective and
true for everybody. But Christianity says, on the contrary,
God has revealed the truth in Jesus Christ who said, 'I am
the way, the Truth and the life.' Now if we are loyal to
the uniqueness and finality of Jesus Christ, however gracious and gentle we may be, I tell you, friends, we
will suffer for it. We will suffer more and more as pluralism and post-modernity grow in many cultures in the
world.

3) The gospel demands holiness. Not as the grounds of salvation, but as the evidence of our salvation. It calls us to
surrender to the supreme Lordship of Jesus Christ. It com-
pels us to accept His moral standards. We want Jesus to
oblige us by lowering His moral standards for our benefit.
We want to set our own standards and resent having to
submit to His.

So here are three gospel stumbling blocks: the freeness of the
gospel, the exclusiveness of the gospel and the high moral
demands of the gospel. Each is an offence to human pride
and arouses people's opposition. I quote from the great
Bonhoeffer in his book *The Cost of Discipleship.* He was a
Lutheran pastor during the Second World War, imprisoned
because of his complicity in the attempt on Hitler's life and
later executed in April 1945. He knew what suffering meant
and he wrote, 'Suffering is the badge of the true Christian.'
It's an amazing statement. You know what a badge is. We all
wear a badge to indicate what society we belong to. If you
want to indicate that you belong to the Society of Jesus,
what is the badge? Answer: suffering. The disciple is not
above his Master.

Luther reckoned suffering among the marks of a true
church. One of the memoranda drawn up in preparation for
the Augsburg Confession similarly defines the church – 'a
community of those who are persecuted and martyred for the
sake of the gospel'. Discipleship means allegiance to the suffering Christ and it is therefore not at all surprising that
Christians should be called upon to suffer. Another Lutheran
pastor, Niemöller, said, 'If a church is not a persecuted church

it ought to ask itself whether it is a church at all.' We need to ask ourselves if we are ready to accept and experience these amazing things in our own lives.

Finally, pastors are:

4) The fathers of the church family (14–21)

In the chapter's final paragraph the apostle calls the Corinthians 'his dear children' (v. 14), in which case he must be their father. He says he is writing to warn them but not to shame them. In verse 15 he adds that although they may have ten thousand guardians or disciplinarians or tutors who will discipline them, they don't have many fathers to love them. Whereas, he has become their spiritual father in Christ and through the gospel and he urges them to imitate him, telling them in verse 17 that he is sending Timothy to them and they are to listen to Timothy and imitate him.

Now this claim of Paul, to be the spiritual father of the Corinthian church, troubles and perplexes many Bible students, because Jesus told us, in Matthew 23:9, not to call anybody our father. Of course we all have, or have had, a father in our home. But he is saying we are not to call anybody our father in the church. Paul does call himself a father. So is Paul contradicting Jesus? No, indeed he isn't. He is not doing what Jesus told us not to do. Jesus was telling us not to adopt towards anybody in the church, and not to require anybody to adopt towards us in the church, the dependent attitude in the relationship of a little child to a father. Christians are to grow up and become interdependent. There are to be no gurus in the Christian community, no teachers in the Confucian mould whose authority is unchallengeable; no tribal chiefs as in Africa. Jesus was forbidding us to assume the authority of a father. But Paul is referring to a father's affection for his children, so he is not contradicting Jesus. Indeed, in 1 Thessalonians 2:5, he likens himself to a mother with her babies, as well as a father. It's a beautiful picture of the love, gentleness and self-sacrifice of a pastor in loving the flock like a father or a mother.

Now of course there is still a place for discipline in the church, which needs to be exercised collectively, as in 1 Corinthians 5. But what is the authentic characteristic of the Christian pastor or leader? Not severity, but gentleness. We are to be fathers and mothers towards those we are called to serve, we are not to be stern disciplinarians whom they fear. And Paul asks the Corinthians, 'What do you prefer? Shall I come to you with a whip [symbol of authority and discipline], or in love and with a gentle spirit?' (v. 21). He leaves this question unanswered because it is up to the Corinthians to reply and to choose.

As I travel in different parts of the world and observe the church and church leaders, I have become convinced that there is too much autocracy and not enough gentleness. There are too many gurus; too many autocrats who lay down the law in the local church in defiance of the teaching of Jesus; too many who behave as if they believe not in the priesthood of all believers, but in the papacy of all pastors! The great need among Christian leaders is for less autocracy and more affection and gentleness. In his book, *The Preacher and his Models* (1891), James Stalker wrote:

> When I was first settled in a church I discovered a thing which nobody had told me and which I had not anticipated. I fell in love with my congregation. I do not know how otherwise to express it. It was as genuine a blossom of the heart as any which I had ever experienced and it made it easy for me to do anything for my people.

Conclusion

From the four pictures the apostle paints, this is how you should regard church leaders of any kind: we are the underlings of Christ; we are the stewards of revelation; we are the scum of the earth; we are the fathers and mothers of the church family. And the common denominator of all four is humility: humility before Christ whose subordinates we are; humility before Scripture of which we are the stewards; humility before the world whose opposition we are bound to encounter; humility before the congregation whose members we are to love and serve.

My prayer for you (and I hope your prayer for me), is that God will richly bless whatever ministry it is that He has called us to exercise. And that our ministry may be characterized above all else by what the apostle in 2 Corinthians 10:1 calls 'the humility and the gentleness of Christ'.*

---

* This material will be published in a slightly expanded form by IVP.

Studies in Nehemiah
by Jonathan Lamb

1. Choosing God's Priorities
Nehemiah 1 & 2

When James Galway, the wonderful Irish flautist, was involved in a nearly fatal road accident, he was forced to evaluate what really mattered in his life. This is what he wrote:

> I decided that from now on I would play every concert, cut every record, give every TV programme, as though it were my last. I have come to understand that it is never possible to guess what might happen next; and that the important thing is to make sure that every time I play the flute, my performance is as near perfection and full of true music as God intended, and that I shall not be remembered for a shoddy performance.

It often takes a crisis to force us to weigh up what really matters in life. It might be our health, a bereavement, a personal tragedy – something which God uses to confront us with that basic question, 'What really matters in life?'

It can also be a positive moment of crisis. Some years ago I stood in a small chapel in Keswick and was asked, 'Do you take this woman to be your lawful wedded wife?' I remember the peculiar appropriateness (at least for my wife) of the text on the wall at the front, 'Call upon me in the day of trouble and I will deliver you'! That kind of moment is a serious moment to assess priorities – for richer for poorer, in sickness and in health, as long as you both shall live.

Some people go through life without ever asking the basic question, 'What really matters?' To quote the actress Helena Bonham Carter, 'We're all going to die anyway; so what does it matter so long as you keep a sense of humour and have fun?' That's today's philosophy: eat, drink and be merry, or eat, drink and watch telly, as we paraphrase it nowadays. Perhaps rather more seriously, the columnist Bernard Levin said that he hoped to discover why he had been born before he died!

So let me ask the question: What matters most to you? What really shapes your priorities in life? Is it your family, your bank balance, your career path, a certain relationship? What is it that motivates you?

The book of Nehemiah raises this fundamental question: What are the priorities for God's people? Once we have discovered those priorities, how can we be determinedly faithful in pursuing them? This book is all about energetic purposefulness. It's about seeing what God calls us to do and then being committed to pursue that path. This is extremely relevant because we Christians are constantly tempted to be diverted from those priorities.

We face pressure from our own culture, which increasingly sees religion as something which has to be marginalized and privatized, until the gospel is gradually nudged aside as irrelevant and unimportant; it's simply a hobby for people like us, religious nerds, as we are called these days.

Also there is pressure within the Christian community or even within our own lives. It's very easy for personal comfort and security to matter more than our desire to seek first God's Kingdom.

Self-fulfilment and self-indulgence sap our devotion and distort our priorities. One reason why we came to Keswick is to step back from distractions either in our culture or in our own lives and reflect prayerfully on what really matters.

Here in the book of Nehemiah it was a sense of crisis in 445 BC which provoked Nehemiah and the people of God to assess what really mattered in their personal and community life. They were forced to confront the priorities which were going to shape their national life and their distinctive witness as God's people.

1) The priority of God's call

The book opens with Nehemiah living and working in a foreign land. Artaxerxes is on the throne of Persia and Nehemiah, the Jew, is there in exile, working as a top civil servant for the king. About 140 years earlier there had been a shift in the world balance of power when Nebuchadnezzar, the king of Babylon, had destroyed Egypt, and his armies had moved into Syria and Palestine. Jeremiah, God's man at that moment, kept prophesying to God's people, warning them that unless they turned around from their unfaithfulness, God would send judgement from the north.

They refused to listen, God did judge and the full weight of the Babylonian war machine moved in, crushed Jerusalem, destroyed the walls, and carried the people off into exile. It was the blackest moment in the history of God's people. In due course, Persia became the dominant power, and during this period small groups of exiles began to return to Jerusalem, firstly under Zerubbabel, then under Ezra, when the temple was rebuilt. (Ezra is a companion book to Nehemiah.) But still the city lay in ruins.

Chapter 1 begins with Nehemiah serving in Susa, the winter palace of the Persian kings. And we need to notice two important elements in the priority of God's call on this man's life.

a) Responsible service

Nehemiah was born in exile. But like other Jews before him, such as Daniel and his friends, Mordecai and Esther, Nehemiah rose to a significant position of influence, in his case, as a prominent civil servant in the court of King Artaxerxes. As he modestly says, 'I was cupbearer to the King' (1:11).

It's impossible to know what that responsibility really meant. Most think it included choosing and tasting the king's wine to check it wasn't poisoned. But he wasn't just a fall guy. He would have close access to the king as his protector and confidant. Xerxes, the father of Artaxerxes, was murdered in his bedroom by one of his courtiers, and so for Nehemiah to have been in this position means he must have been trusted as one of the top officials in Susa. Notice that Nehemiah's position and training in that pagan court was part of God's work in his life, equipping him for the challenge which lay ahead.

When he heard the distressing news of what was happening in his home city, Nehemiah was ideally placed to take action. There was no dramatic 'call', no divine vision and no angelic messenger. He wasn't a religious professional, priest, or prophet, he was a civil servant for a pagan king 700 miles away from home. But here was a man whom God could trust, whose priorities were clear, and who was going to be central to God's work of rebuilding his people.

Mark Greene, from the London Institute of Contemporary Christianity, reminds us that there are about 4 million Christians in Britain, but only 100,000 Christian ministers. 'If we want to win Britain it will be done by equipping the 4 million for ministry wherever God places them. We will do it when the 4 million are equipped to bring biblical values to bear in discussions in offices and boardrooms and factories and hospitals.'

Every Christian should be ready to take the opportunities right where God has placed them, to live for Jesus Christ in the now, not just in some hoped-for future. If you find yourself asking, 'What on earth am I doing in this office?' it is important to see that Nehemiah was committed to responsible service right where God had placed him. Away from home, in a pagan court, as a follower of Yahweh, he might often have said, 'What am I doing here?' We need to live for the Lord Jesus, for His kingdom values wherever He has placed us. You are in a unique position to do that.

b) *A responsive heart*

Verse 2 introduces the news which Nehemiah receives from his home town when a group of Jews arrive in Susa, and we gain some insight about Nehemiah's concern because they don't volunteer the information:

> … I questioned them about the Jewish remnant that survived the exile, and also about Jerusalem. They said to me, 'Those who survived the exile and are back in the province are in

great trouble and disgrace. The wall of Jerusalem is broken
down, and its gates have been burned with fire.' When I
heard these things, I sat down and wept. For some days I
mourned and fasted and prayed before the God of heaven
(1:2–3).

The news was overwhelming and had a deep emotional and
spiritual impact on Nehemiah. The message was clear: God's
work was paralysed and God's people were demoralized.
It's most likely that this was the result of the king's order to
cease rebuilding: 'They compelled the Jews by force to stop'
(Ezr. 4:23). It was a shattering blow for Nehemiah, not simply because of the disgrace of God's people, but because of
what this represented: God was being dishonoured. Jerusalem was to be a 'dwelling for his name' (Neh. 1:9), it was the
holy city, it was the place where His presence would be specially known. Now, instead of its distinctive witness to God's
glory and honour, instead of it being a light to the nations, it
had become 'an international joke', as one commentator
puts it.

Nehemiah might have had a responsible job in Susa, with
considerable security and prosperity, but he hadn't lost his
spiritual passion. It's all too easy for us to lose our spiritual
edge, to be indifferent about God's honour, but not
Nehemiah. Such was his concern for God's name and God's
honour, he mourned and fasted and prayed (v. 4).

In his account of the recent war in Bosnia, war correspon-
dent Anthony Lloyd indicates how easy it is to become
de-sensitized to the appalling results of such inhumanity:

> Brutal mutilation would stick in my eyes like a thorn for days,
> or else the expression or posture of a corpse would evoke sad-
> ness and anger within me. But as you lose count of the num-
> ber of dead you have seen, a hidden threshold of sensitivity is
> raised, neutralising most of your reactions.

That's what happens to us Christians: our reactions to the
appalling spiritual and moral decline which we see around us
are neutralized. We are living in a culture which has rejected
God, but who would dream of even suggesting that we should
dwell on, let alone weep over, the evil in our own hearts or the

evil in our society or the spiritual decline we see in the church? Evangelicalism has very little place for tears.

We have to ask, how do we feel about the liberalism of the church? or the fractured evangelicalism? or the declining influence of God's people in society? or the rampant religious pluralism? There are now more Muslims in the UK than there are communicant members of the Church of England. How do we feel about the fact that people are not worshipping Jesus?

When one of General Booth's workers was struggling to see any success in his work with the Salvation Army, he sent a telegram to Booth asking for advice. He received a reply, which contained just two words: 'Try tears.'

It was that kind of responsive heart that was to be a foundation priority in God's calling of Nehemiah and it is a foundation priority in our calling too – responsible service where God has placed us and a responsive heart to what God wants to do in the desperate situation in which we sometimes find ourselves.

2) The priority of God's purposes

'For some days I mourned and fasted and prayed before the God of heaven' (v. 4). One of the most significant features of the book of Nehemiah is the frequent reference to his praying. Chuck Swindoll calls Nehemiah 'a leader from the knees up'. His dependence on God was a vital priority in determining God's purposes for the work ahead. He is certainly an activist who got things done and yet his first reaction on hearing the news was to commit himself to weeks of prayer.

What a lesson for our personal lives and our churches. When we confront a challenge we are sometimes governed more by the maxim, 'Why pray when you can worry?' He had received devastating news and his godliness is reflected in the fact that he was committed first to discover the priority of God's purposes. There was nothing else he could do. No one but God could accomplish what needed to be done, one man faced that huge task. If there is one great value in facing desperate situations where we have no idea what to do or how to respond, it is that we are forced to hold fast to God.

Abraham Lincoln expressed it like this: 'I have been driven many times to my knees by the overwhelming conviction that I had nowhere else to go. My own wisdom and that of those about me seemed insufficient for the day.' Nowhere else to go other than to God Himself. That's just how Nehemiah felt and it is a basic attitude we need to cultivate right through our Christian life and especially in our praying.

Christians face a subtle temptation: we would like to think that we fulfil God's purposes unaided. The book of Nehemiah is shot through with examples of this man's dependence on God, his devotion to God, his submission to God, and his desire for the glory of God, and in the end nowhere else to go. Verse 5 introduces us to a model of how to pray in a desperate situation. Nehemiah places the present challenge in the context of God's history of relating to his people with a mosaic of biblical references that form the foundation for his requests. There is great value in praying like this.

Let's look at three features of the prayer:

a) The powerful God who fulfils His plans (1:5)

'O Lord, God of heaven, the great and awesome God, who keeps his covenant of love' (v. 5). 'O Lord, God of heaven' – that's always the place to begin. The Lord, Yahweh, the personal God, the God of the Exodus who had saved his people, 'whom you redeemed by your great strength and your mighty hand' (v. 10), and defeated their enemies. The God of heaven: the Sovereign Lord who has universal supremacy. The transcendent Creator. The God, above all other 'godlets' (A. Motyer) who has the power to fulfil his purposes (see 2:4; 20; 8:6; 1:5; 4:14; 9:32).

For Nehemiah, this wasn't theory. For the job he had to do this needed to be in his bones, in his heart. He says this great and awesome God is 'my God' – a phrase which appears ten times in his memoirs. In the building programme he was to lead, in the opposition he was to confront, in the reforms he was to introduce, he would depend on 'my God' at every turn, trusting the great and awesome God. And the reason for his dogged determination against all odds was that, like Moses, 'he persevered because he saw him who is invisible' (Heb. 11:27).

I often work amongst Christians in countries where the evangelical community is a desperately small minority, where human and financial resources are minuscule, and where the temptation to give up is a daily one. Some of us feel like this and in such circumstances we need to be able to 'see' the Lord, Yahweh, the God of heaven, the great and awesome God. It certainly makes a difference to the way we pray, if first of all we raise our eyes to the great and awesome God, the God above all other 'godlets.

b) *The faithful God who keeps His promises* (1:5, 8, 9)

> ...who keeps his covenant of love. (v. 5)

> Remember the instruction you gave your servant Moses, saying, 'If you are unfaithful, I will scatter you among the nations, but if you return to me and obey my commands, then even if your exiled people are at the farthest horizon, I will gather them from there and bring them to the place I have chosen as a dwelling for my Name' (vv. 8, 9)

One of the most distinctive ideas in the Old Testament is God's steady persistence in loving His people despite their extraordinary waywardness. That's what He promised, and he'll remain faithful to that promise. The Bible uses the word 'covenant' to describe that relationship and Nehemiah's prayer is based on that foundation: God can be trusted. God will be faithful to what He has promised. His covenants in the Old Testament were founded on His sovereign grace. He had chosen the Jews, He had revealed himself to them, He had rescued them and therefore He would not give up on them. So Nehemiah prays in verse 8, 'Remember.' It's a key word in the book of Nehemiah (4:14; 5:19; 6:14; 13:14, 22,29,31) and it represented a call to God to intervene. He's saying, 'If you've been faithful to your promise in sending us into exile because of our unfaithfulness, now fulfil your promise to bring us back and restore us, as we obey you.'

The same theme comes through in the prayer of chapter 9:8, 32, 33, which is saturated with that kind of covenant language – *your* people, *our* God, *my* God. We belong to You. Please be faithful in fulfilling what you have promised, 'Restore, O Lord, the honour of your name.'

There are many times when we feel we cannot pray because we are paralysed by our sense of failure. We can't imagine that God would listen to us, let alone accept us back. It's then that these words matter: 'You keep your covenant of love.' However inadequate my faith, however slight my hold of Him, God will not let go of me. We need to remember that the greatest covenant of all is found in Jesus Christ. By faith in Him we have been brought into a covenant relationship with the living God and with His global family, founded on God's grace. So when we pray, however inadequate that might be, we can come to God on the basis of His having chosen us, having welcomed us into His family, having saved us through Christ's work.

We say the same as Nehemiah – we belong to You; please don't give up on us; be faithful in keeping Your promises. And that's why praying with the Bible in our hands is so important. When I feel paralysed in my praying I turn to a prayer like this, or to some of the psalms to appeal to God. Spurgeon used to say when he found it difficult to pray, 'We shall find every attribute of the Most High to be, as it were, a great battering ram with which we may open the gates of heaven.' Whatever our emotional or spiritual state, we can come to God knowing that His grace never ends. He is the faithful God who keeps His promises.

c) The holy God who requires obedience (1:5–7)

who keeps his covenant of love with those who love him and obey his commands. (v. 5)

I confess the sins we Israelites, including myself and my father's house, have committed against you. We have acted very wickedly toward you. We have not obeyed the commands, decrees and laws you gave your servant Moses. (vv. 6, 7)

Having reviewed God's covenant promises, Nehemiah moves to confession. This was also a covenant of human responsibility: obedience to God mattered. The judgement of God, that had resulted in the destruction of Jerusalem, was the result of their sin. So it follows that, if he was about to appeal to God for the restoration of the city and its people, it would have to be done on the basis of a confession of those sins which had led to its destruction.

Nehemiah doesn't distance himself, he identifies with the people and acknowledges his own sinfulness before God. There is nothing self-righteous or superior about him. Ezra was much the same. Discovering the unfaithfulness of the people, he prayed, 'O my God, I am too ashamed and disgraced to lift up my face to you, my God, because our sins are higher than our heads and our guilt has reached to the heavens' (Ezr. 9:6). This kind of solidarity is important. It's all too easy to criticize the church or distance ourselves from its failings, but when the Holy Spirit is at work He will show us that we too are guilty.

If mourning over the state of our church and our country is one of the lessons of this chapter, then coming in confession to a holy God, who requires obedience, is part of that process. Nehemiah would only know God's blessing as he and the people expressed genuine repentance for their unfaithfulness. One of the features most noted in accounts of revival is this awareness of the awfulness of sin and a willingness to confront it in prayerful repentance. As we confront the challenge of God's Word and allow the Holy Spirit to review our attitudes, our behaviour, our habits, our motivations and our priorities, we too will begin to see sin as God sees it, and respond as Nehemiah did.

Finally, in an attitude of submission, he brings his request at the close of the prayer on the basis of the rock-solid convictions we have highlighted. He has prayed to the powerful God who fulfils His plans, the faithful God who keeps His promises and the holy God who requires obedience. Now, in the context of renewed commitment, Nehemiah lays his specific request before God: 'O Lord, let your ear be attentive to the prayer of your servant and to the prayer of your

servants who delight in revering your name. Give your
servant success today by granting him favour in the presence
of this man' (v. 11).

Nehemiah had prayed day and night for months. What
shaped the future was neither his diplomacy, nor his political
or administrative skill, it was seeking for God's purposes.

3) The priority of God's perspective

A story is told of an Oxford undergraduate who, at the end of
his final year, wrote a letter to his parents:

Dear Mum and Dad,

*I know you haven't heard much from me in recent months, but the fact
is this. A few weeks back, there was a fire in the flat and I lost all my
possessions. In fact I only escaped with my life by jumping out of a
second-floor window. In the process of doing so I broke my leg, so I
finished up in hospital. Fortunately, I met the most wonderful nurse
there. We immediately fell in love, and, well, to cut a long story short,
last Saturday we got married. Many of our friends say this was
over-hasty, but I am convinced that our love will more than
compensate for the differences between our social backgrounds and
ethnic origins.*

*By this time, Mum and Dad, I suspect you may be getting a bit
worried, so let me tell you straight away that everything I have written in this letter up to now is false. I made it up.*

*The truth is, two weeks ago I failed my final exams. I just want
you to get this in the proper perspective.*

Nehemiah was concerned to gain the proper perspective on
the problems that lay ahead and I do believe that for many of
us in our Christian calling, in our work, in our families, aiming
to understand a proper perspective is vital.

a) God's timing (2:1–9)

Chapter 2 opens after four months of Nehemiah mourning,
fasting and praying. Gradually he had come to the point of
formulating his prayer request of 1:11. Everything now
depended on God's timing. Nehemiah was an activist and his

willingness to wait for God's time to answer the prayer is
impressive. Any premature action on his part would have
threatened the entire venture.

Weeks passed until eventually, one day, king Artaxerxes
asked Nehemiah why he appeared so sad (v. 2). Appearing
mournful before the king was worthy of punishment, and
commentators vary as to whether he deliberately decided this
was the day to look mournful or whether, given the four
months of fasting and mourning, it was inevitable that eventually the king would see the physical and emotional deteriora-
tion. Either way, Nehemiah was ready to respond to the
questioning of the king. Look at his carefully crafted answer:
'May the King live forever! Why should my face not look sad
when the city where my fathers are buried lies in ruins, and its
gates have been burned with fire?' (Neh. 2:3) So when the king
then asked, 'What is it you want?' he was ready to describe
everything he needed to do the job of going back to Jerusalem,
rebuilding the walls and rebuilding the people (verses 5–9).

As well as praying, he had done his homework. He was
dependent on God, but he was also ready to take the initiative.
There is no doubt that for many of us the 'waiting times' are
the most demanding periods of Christian discipleship. And for
anyone with an activist mentality, these four months of determining what might be God's will and when to act could have
been a form of torture. But this is often the pathway God calls
us to walk. Too often we imagine that prayer will provide us
with a quick-fix solution.

The process of prayer is one whereby we begin to think
God's thoughts after Him, to desire the things He desires,
love the things He loves. It is a process whereby we begin to
see things from His point of view. The waiting time is often
when God can make us what he wants us to be. This had
been happening during Nehemiah's four months of prayer.
And it is in this context that his famous arrow prayer should
be seen. 'Then I prayed to the God of heaven and answered
the king' (Neh. 2:4). Nehemiah knew 'my God' and was able
to discern immediately that this was the moment for action.

The fact that it was God's time is clearly signalled in verse
8: 'And because the gracious hand of my God was upon me,

the king granted my requests.' And it must have been God's hand. The decision to allow Nehemiah to return and rebuild Jerusalem required the king to make a political U-turn. He had previously ordered that the rebuilding work should stop (Ezr. 4:15, 21). Now he had to reverse his foreign policy.

It's possible that the unstable political situation of the time meant that Artaxerxes saw the wisdom of strengthening Judah, providing a buffer state between his Persia and a rather unstable Egypt. But even if it was a wise political move, it was still the hand of God. Recently, following the intervention of the Norwegian Defence Minster, who is a believer, the president of Azerbaijan completely reversed his clampdown on religious freedom, releasing pastors and granting a request to build a church. It was complete U-turn. God is well able to do this.

There was much prayer and political intervention, but ultimately all of those concerned could say, along with Ezra and Nehemiah, 'the gracious hand of my God was upon me' (see also Ezr. 7:6, 9, 28; 8:18; Neh. 2:18). It was the Lord, the God of heaven, who could cause the autocratic king of Persia to reverse his former foreign policy, and He is able to do that in the details of your life and mine, as well as in international politics.

Many Christians struggle with the bewildering questions surrounding the impact of evil, the opposition against the churches, the apparent delays in God's action in our family, or personal life, but in such circumstances we need to hold on to the priority of God's timing. He knows what is best. As Peter was to say to the hard-pressed believers of his day, 'The Lord is not slow in keeping his promise... The day of the Lord will come...' (2 Pet. 3:9, 10).

b) God's control (2:10–20)

Gaining God's perspective is vital in every area of our lives. We can be overcome with pessimism and discouragement, or ignore the challenges and dismiss the opposition. We need to see things as they are and see things as they could be.

Within a matter of days of arriving in Jerusalem,

Nehemiah says, 'By night I went out through the Valley Gate toward the Jackal Wall and the Dung gate, examining the walls of Jerusalem, which had been broken down, and its gates, which had been destroyed by fire' (v. 13). He was carefully assessing the need. He didn't rush into action, he wanted to be realistic about the challenge that lay ahead.

With the circumference of the walls having been estimated at about two miles, the destruction was considerable. Massive stones that had tumbled down into the valley, blocking his way on horseback (v. 14), needed to be reassembled.

He was counting the cost before building the tower and that is part of the process in any work God calls us to do. Such a perspective is also realistic about the opposition to God's work which we will always encounter as God's people. Nehemiah has hinted at this in 2:10. He was in danger of upsetting the balance of power. Judah's neighbours had a vested interest in keeping Jerusalem weak. They would face direct confrontation, but the work they were to be engaged in was the work of God. And this is the shift of perspective we need when we are disheartened by the rubble or intimidated by the opposition. Nehemiah says to his fellow workers, ' "You see the trouble we are in: Jerusalem lies in ruins, and its gates have been burned with fire. Come, let us rebuild the wall of Jerusalem and we will no longer be in disgrace." I also told them about the gracious hand of my God upon me and what the king had said to me.' (vv. 17, 18). 'The God of heaven will give us success' (v. 20).

He urges them to see things as they could be. He creates what we might call 'godly expectation': the God-given ability to see what could be, rather than just what is. This is basic to our work for God. George Carey calls a lack of vision 'an ecclesiastical terminal illness'. The dispirited people in Jerusalem needed more than the power of positive thinking. Their hearts and minds needed lifting to see what God could do. And we are the same. We need to be dissatisfied with where we are and develop a lively expectation of what, by God's grace, could be in our lives, in our churches, in our cause or mission.

Nehemiah was to turn them from 'the trouble and disgrace'

(1:3 and 2:17) towards the 'gracious hand of our God' (2:18). This attitude encourages 'old men to dream dreams, and young men to see visions'. It is Joshua saying to the people, 'Get ready, you will cross the Jordan'; it is Nehemiah saying, 'Come, let's rebuild the wall of Jerusalem.' The critical turning point in the change of perspective was to see that God was behind the project. 'The God of heaven will give us success' (v. 20). This is the fundamental priority we need in our own service for the Lord: it is God's work. It was the great missionary pioneer, Hudson Taylor, who said: 'It's not great faith we need but faith in a great God.'

2. Building God's People
Nehemiah 3 & 5

Recently I met a Polish man who was living in Australia and working in Asia. 'I have no idea who I am or where I belong,' he told me. This is probably one of the most common complaints, not only in today's youth culture, but with people of all ages. There is a deep crisis of belonging. Many factors have contributed to this disorientation and rootlessness, but one of the most significant is the fracture of social relationships of all kinds.

In his book on *Love and Friendship* the American social commentator, Allan Bloom, says, 'Isolation, a sense of lack of profound contact with other human beings, seems to be the disease of our time.' In a recent survey when university students were asked to identify their number one problem, 80 per cent replied, 'Loneliness.'

By the end of this year, 60 per cent of us will have mobile phones in the UK. One forecaster comments that, 'Mobiles do not reflect liberation but loneliness. Once people belonged to things and believed in things, now if they are lonely they just have their phones. Giving them the impression of belonging to a network provides security.' In less than 15 years' time it is estimated that in more than 30 per cent of British households, there will be a solitary person, 7.6 million separate units ('civic atoms').

And we need hardly add to this the statistics of divorce. Globally, in one hour, 2000 couples will marry, 1300 couples will divorce. Few of us are spared the pain of fractured relationships. The sense of emotional isolation and social alienation is a daily reality for many of us. Even as Christians we sometimes feel that deep, in-your-bones loneliness.

It's no wonder, then, that those who wish to encourage the church in its task of mission urge us to reflect on the importance of one over-arching biblical theme: community. To understand and live by the biblical teaching on true community will today be counter-cultural. And if we live as we should as God's people, it will be deeply attractive in this world of social alienation.

God's covenant formula, 'I will be your God, you will be my people', is repeated throughout the Old Testament, and is expressed in the New Testament in the reality of God's church, God's new society; this is the place where true community should be expressed.

We sometimes look at the book of Nehemiah as a wonderful book about leadership. And so it is. But it would be a mistake to view it solely as the story of an individual. Its underlying theme is not so much the importance of leadership, nor the importance of the building of a wall, it is a story about the restoration of God's people, God's community. Chapters 8 to 13 express this in a variety of ways. In chapters 7, 10, 11, 12 we find quite long lists of people, identifying who their ancestors were and which village they came from. This was all part of the process of defining identity and strengthening solidarity as God's community now they are back from exile.

Let us focus on two main themes:

1) The community at work (chapter 3)

The task of rebuilding the wall was to become a major community enterprise. Just as important as repairing and rebuilding the wall and the gates of the city, the experience itself would bring together the fragmented community in Jerusalem. Chapter 3 reveals several significant features of community building which are worth highlighting. They each have their contemporary parallel as we reflect on this issue: how do we build Christian community today?

a) A shared purpose

It's worth remembering that the exile had been a devastating blow for God's people. The destruction of the temple, the collapse of the city, the evacuation of the people − all of those events had called into question their status as the people of God. So the building programme which begins here in chapter 3 is, in reality, the beginning of the rebuilding of the shattered community, the people who belonged to God.

Rebuilding the walls would have several effects. Firstly, it would be a testimony to God's power, as we have seen in Nehemiah's motivational speech in chapter 2:20, 'The God of heaven will give us success.' But secondly, it expressed their determination to be holy, distinct, separated from other nations in their faithfulness to God. Gordon McGonville points out the importance of the walls as 'symbols'. 'Walls, like flags, can provide identity and solidarity. It is in these terms that we should view the present activity. The Lord was giving his people a badge, a further token − alongside the temple − that they *were* his people.'

And what is clear, as we read chapter 3, is the sense of solidarity, the shared purpose, the *esprit de corps*. They were working together wholeheartedly, they weren't just clearing rubble and carting rocks, they were concerned with something far greater. The story is told of the foreman on a building site who asks one of the builders what he is doing and he replies, 'I'm breaking rocks.' Then he asks the second man: 'I'm earning for my family,' he replies. When he comes to the third, with a glint in his eye, he replies, 'I'm building a cathedral.' You will know the object of your work radically affects the way in which you work. If you are inspired you can put up with almost any inconvenience, overcome almost any obstacle.

For the people in chapter 3, building the walls was a testimony. This was a special city. Nehemiah had wept at the news of the disgrace of the broken city in chapter 1. Now, the rebuilding of the walls was a reflection of God's glory. It was His city. It was His name that was to dwell there (1:9).

The shared purpose is acknowledged early on in the rebuilding programme. 'Eliashib the high priest and his fellow priests went to work and rebuilt the Sheep Gate' (3:1). Up in the north-east corner this gate provided easy access to the temple and probably took its name from the sheep coming in for sacrifice. It is significant that Nehemiah began the work here, led by the priests, close to the temple. And the verse continues: 'They dedicated it'. They consecrated this section of the work to God's glory. And when the wall was completed they celebrated its entire dedication, with marching and singing (12:27).

This was not just a construction activity – 'the people worked with all their heart' (4:6). They had a shared purpose in their hearts, they knew this was God's work and it was for God's glory. That inspired them, that motivated their muscles, that pushed them forward in the rebuilding work.

In the twenty-first century, our circumstances are entirely different. However, the principle here is extremely relevant to the building of Christian community. The effectiveness of the church's mission depends, in no small degree, on this kind of corporate solidarity and shared purpose focused around the Lord Jesus. As Paul says in Ephesians 2:21, in his metaphor of building, 'In him the whole building is joined together and rises to become a holy temple in the Lord and in him you too are being built together to become a dwelling in which God lives by his Spirit.'

This kind of solidarity is constantly under attack and all churches face the challenge of how to 'maintain the unity of the Spirit in the bonds of peace'. One of the primary objectives of Satan is to attack this sense of shared purpose amongst Christians. He will do his utmost to disrupt any work of God by moving people away from their unified intention to do God's work for God's glory and will induce various forms of self-defeating chaos. It might be the smallest of things: disagreements over the colour you paint the walls of the church building, over the hymnbook you use, or the way the seats should be put out, or whether the Mother and Toddler group can use the baptistry as a sand pit! We are deflected from the primary task for all kinds of reasons.

True Christian community will be strengthened when our purpose is clear, and we work together wholeheartedly to achieve it. We need:

b) A co-operative spirit

As you read through the memoirs you get a general impression that all kinds of people are drawn together in achieving one purpose. Throughout the chapter there are phrases such as 'next to him', 'next to them', and each person worked 'side by side', irrespective of their background. Paul says in Ephesians that we are all members of one family with one Father, indwelt by the one Holy Spirit, redeemed by the one Lord Jesus Christ. So how do all these cogs mesh together?

The list in chapter 3 shows that 40 different sections of the wall were worked on by people from different family units, different towns, different trades and professions, different genders, temple servants, district officials, priests and Levites. Nehemiah walks right round the walls and records that 'the goldsmiths and the merchants' (v. 32) were working alongside the priests at the Sheep Gate (v. 1).

At certain points, Nehemiah clearly delegates responsibility to others, trusting them to oversee their section. 'Next to him, the repairs were made by the Levites under Rehum son of Bani. Beside him, Hashabiah, ruler of the half district of Keilah, carried out repairs for his district' (3:17).

This sort of team effort was essential to get the job done, and almost everyone rolled up their sleeves and was willing to get their hands dirty.

I saw a poster recently, which read: 'Teamwork – means never having to take all the blame yourself!' Teamwork is basic to all Christian service. It is essential in any church that we create a sense of community ownership. Leaders are called to equip others for their work of ministry, as Paul demonstrates in Ephesians 4. Every person, whatever their occupation, whatever their background, whatever their gender, is called in the mobilization of God's people.

The ministry of mobilizing all of God's people is very much needed in our churches. It has been estimated that in the average church 90 per cent of the work is done by 10 per cent of the people. In the church there are thousands of spectators in the stands who badly need some exercise, and a small team of men and women on the field who badly need a rest!

The New Testament emphasis on Christian community calls for every-member ministry, a total participation of all those who are committed to the Lord of the church. Each person finding their place on the wall, whatever their background, occupation, or gender, however young or old a believer they may be. Working with that rich diversity to serve with their God-given gifts. The purpose of leaders is to multiply not to monopolize ministry (see Eph. 4:16). How to liberate God's people in our churches is a very important part of the work God is calling us to do.

c) Committed leadership

Along with the high priest and his fellow priests, several other community leaders and rulers are involved in the construction of the wall. That kind of leadership from the front is essential. The only discordant note in the chapter comes in verse 5, 'The next section was repaired by the men of Tekoa, but their nobles would not put their shoulders to the work under their supervisors.' Hugh Williamson notes that the verse could literally be read, 'They did not bring their necks into service … the image is suggestive of pride ('stiff necked') rather than lack of enthusiasm.' It was not simply that such work was beneath them. These particular nobles clearly resented Nehemiah's leadership. They had failed to capture the spirit of the enterprise: God's work for God's glory, and were more interested in personal status.

This attitude of the nobles is found in the church too. And again it works against true community. It's found in a spirit of competition, or of status-seeking, or envy. Paul describes some of the attitudes he faced in Philippians 1. Some people were characterized by *envy* (v. 15): they couldn't stand someone being more successful than they were. And then there was *rivalry* (v. 15): they enjoyed belittling the work of others, imagining Christian work was a competition. And finally *self-ish ambition* (v. 17): the word has the flavour of canvassing for political office.

These people weren't interested in the advance of the Kingdom, but in establishing the power base for their own work. This kind of church politics is pretty ugly. But Paul was able to rise above it. He was not concerned with prestige or personal glory. 'The important thing,' he said, 'is that Christ is preached.' That's the kind of committed leadership we need to display. Not my reputation, my status, my position, my denomination, but the cause of Christ.

2) The community at risk (chapter 5)

Nehemiah now records an internal issue, which could have had very serious consequences not just for the life of the community but also for its witness to the surrounding nations. The whole enterprise of rebuilding the wall would have been of little worth, if at the same time the people themselves had not been rebuilt into the true community of God.

What was the problem?

a) Destructive inequality (5:1–5)

v. 1. Notice that this was within the family, in the community. The men and their wives raised 'a great outcry against their Jewish brothers; "we are of the same flesh and blood as our countrymen ... but..."' (v. 5). Something was happening which had the potential to create fracture lines and blow them apart. It focused around an economic crisis and the opening verses show that there were three complaints surfacing:

v. 2. Some of those working on the wall were poor. They owned no land and had no source of income whilst they were in Jerusalem, engaged in the building project, and so their families were gradually starving.

v. 3. A second group is identified. They did have property, but they had to hand it over to finance houses, mortgaging their fields and vineyards and homes in order to pay for the increasing cost of food while they faced the added pressure of famine.

v. 4. A third group was having to borrow money in order to pay the taxes demanded by the king.

v. 5. Such was the hardship, some families were having to sell their children into debt-slavery. 'Some of our daughters have already been enslaved, but we are powerless' – the word 'enslaved' could even have overtones of sexual abuse. The creditors were fellow countrymen, the same flesh and blood.

Here we see the classic spiral decline into the poverty trap. And what caused the outcry was the fact that the community, that was to be known by God's name and was to declare God's values, was characterized by injustice and exploitation, in the midst of this building project. In fact, it was not one community, it was two communities: the exploiters and the exploited, the powerful and the disadvantaged. It is quite a contrast to the shared purpose and co-operative spirit in chapter 3, or the collective strength seen in chapter 4. Now something has happened which is tearing this community apart. I think it was Alec Motyer who commented on hypocritical Christians, 'praying on their knees on Sunday and preying on their neighbours on Monday'. Well, that's how it felt here.

To set it into context, in terms of what the law permitted, the creditors were not acting illegally. But in the context of true community, the spirit of the law demanded something different. They were using a legal technique to redeem land for their own greedy benefit, and were exploiting impoverished people who were part of their own community.

The simple point of application is this: selfishness and greed are enormously destructive of true community. The Old Testament prophets brought out their 'big guns' to condemn these attitudes and practices. They recognized that greed, oppression and injustice destroyed families and community. Poverty and debt led to appalling divisions amongst God's people. That's what led to the distressing cry, 'we are powerless' (v. 5). As Chris Wright comments in his book on the ethical authority of the Old Testament, 'This is a cry with some very modern echoes.'

In the New Testament greed was not seen as some private vice. We tend to think what we do with our possessions is our own business. In 1 Corinthians 5:10, 11 Paul lists the offenders who are to be excluded from the church. All of them have committed public or community offences – sexual immorality, idolatry, slander, drunkeness, swindling, which are corporate in their impact. He then speaks about the greedy person who refused to do good within the family of believers. 'As we have opportunity, let us do good to all people, especially to those who belong to the family of believers' (Gal. 6:10).

The attitude which insists on personal gain, but has no heart for the needs of others, is incompatible with the true sense of belonging amongst God's people, whether in the Old Testament, the New Testament or today's church.

b) Serious inconsistency (5:7–9)

Nehemiah highlights the internal inconsistency of such behaviour within the community. 'You are exacting usury from your own countrymen!' (v. 7). 'These are your brothers! They're members of the family!' He describes with more than a hint of irony in verse 8, another element which is self-contradictory. 'You are selling your brothers only for them to be sold back to us!'.

The Jews were committed to do all they could to buy back their family members who had been sold into slavery to the Gentiles. They paid a redemption price in order to set them free. And now, after all of the efforts to buy back family members from foreigners, the creditors were setting up a new form of slavery, actually within the community itself.

There was a serious internal inconsistency and Nehemiah's memoir states it succinctly: 'They kept quiet, because they could find nothing to say' (v. 8).

Nehemiah presses his point still further, 'So I continued, "What you are doing is not right. Shouldn't you walk in the fear of our God to avoid the reproach of our Gentile enemies?"' (v. 9).

The inconsistency within the community was clear. But what about the message it is giving to people outside the community? There was an external inconsistency. Nehemiah is speaking once again about the honour of God's name. How the community behaved reflected on God himself. Nations around Judah would look at her behaviour and draw conclusions about the God whom they worshipped. Their community life was intended to be a radical challenge to the nations round about. So Nehemiah was right to imply that injustice, selfishness, greed − a lack of generosity and solidarity in community − invited criticism by the Gentiles and reflected badly on the name and reputation of God Himself.

And of course the same applies today. Any form of division within Christian community not only impacts fellowship internally, but damages our credibility in the eyes of a watching world. Once a minister was asked if he had an active congregation. 'Oh yes,' he replied, 'half of them are working with me and half of them are working against me!' He chose a humorous way to highlight a serious problem. Some 350 years ago Richard Baxter wrote: 'The public takes note of all this division and not only derides us, but becomes hardened against all religion. When we try to persuade them, they see so many factions that they do not know which to join and think it is better not to join any of them. Thus thousands grow in contempt of all religion by our divisions.'

There is a massive credibility gap when we affirm our unity and community and yet fail to demonstrate it in the realities of our lives. And whilst this applies generally to the way we live as God's people, there is also the specific application of this passage to the issues of social and economic justice within the community.

In his recent book on the religion of greed, Brian Rosner records how, in the second century, a converted Greek philosopher attempted to characterize Christians of his day, constructing a profile which demonstrated that Christians lived differently from the pagans around them in three ways.

1) They didn't practise idolatry.
2) They didn't practise sexual immorality.
3) 'If they see a stranger, they bring him under their roof. If they hear that any of their number is imprisoned or oppressed ... all of them provide for his needs ... And if there is among them a man that is poor and needy ... they fast for two or three days that they may supply the needy with the necessary food.'

Rosner summarizes, 'In the early church, the sharing of possessions was just as central to what it means to be a Christian as are the exclusive worship of the true God and the matter of sexual purity.'

We Christians need to see ourselves, not as a collection of individuals, with our separate priorities and needs, but as members of a community, the body of Christ, with all of its privileges and obligations.

The New Testament emphasis on the gift of hospitality meant more than entertaining one another at dinner parties, it was a commitment to help travellers, to provide somewhere for Christians to meet, and to care practically for the economically disadvantaged. The word 'hospitality' literally meant 'love for the stranger'. I have a friend who defines hospitality as 'making people feel at home when you wish they were!' Of course, this is costly, whether in terms of time or money or inconvenience. But generosity of this kind has a theological basis. You have been accepted by God, welcomed by Him, brought into His family. Now show that same generosity towards others.

So back in Nehemiah 5, it was time for action

c) Honest confrontation (5:10, 14–19)

'I and my brothers and my men are also lending the people money and grain. But let the exacting of usury stop. Give back to them immediately their fields, vineyards, olive groves and houses, and also the usury you are charging them – the hundredth part of the money, grain, new wine and oil.'

'We will give it back', they said. 'And we will not demand anything more from them. We will do as you say' (v. 10).

He is swift to call for the immediate cancellation of debts and interest, and also the return of any property that had been used in repayment. There are two issues here at the personal level, which say something about Nehemiah's leadership in the situation.

Firstly, *personal responsibility.* In verse 10 it is clear that he is honest enough to admit that he too had been involved in the lending of money and grain. He might not have been involved in the extreme exploitation of which others were guilty, but he shows a willingness to confront personal failure and not to hide behind his position. We live in an atmosphere, in our churches, where leaders are not allowed to fail.

Mark Roberts suggests, in his commentary on Nehemiah, that we have grown accustomed to the endless denials and evasions of our political leaders. 'Rather than admit mistakes, they blame just about everyone else – the other political party, or the media, or the Japanese, or their predecessors; rarely do we observe our leaders freely admitting their failures. It seems that "I was wrong" doesn't play too well on the six o'clock news.'

Nehemiah is modelling genuine Christian community. It is a community of grace, a community of the forgiven, and in this environment there should be room for us leaders to acknowledge areas of failure, learning to confront, forgive, and change.

Secondly, *personal example.* Nehemiah's memoirs go further. They not only show his willingness to identify with failure, but also his positive commitment to generosity. Chapter 5:14–19 is another autobiographical section where Nehemiah describes his own motives and actions.

Previous governors of the city, 'placed a heavy burden on the people' (v. 15). This was their due as they ran substantial expense accounts because of their responsibilities. But Nehemiah says, because the people are under such pressure, he will not do that, he will cover the costs himself. He gives two reasons why he didn't take advantage of that facility.

Firstly, 'But out of reverence for God I did not act like that. Instead I devoted myself to the work on this wall' (v. 16). In the light of his commitment to the God who had called him to rebuild the city and the people, he was determined to be different from other governors, those whom he describes as 'lording it over the people' (v. 15).

Secondly, 'I never demanded the food allotted to the governor, because the demands were heavy on these people' (v. 18). It was his sense of brotherly solidarity with the people that meant he refused to place any further burdens on them. He had the right to do so, but he preferred to carry the cost himself rather than add to the burdens of his fellow family members.

You might recognize his two motives from Jesus' simple summing up of the law: love for God who called him to that work and love for others who belonged to Him in this family.

d) Practical solidarity (5:12, 13)

Finally, Nehemiah calls the people to action. As the people agreed with his proposals to give back the land, to take steps to restore equality and to act generously, Nehemiah calls them to take an oath to do what they had promised (vv. 12,13). This was vital for the well-being of the immediate task of building the wall. But more than that, it was basic to what constituted fellowship amongst the people of God. Community was the place of belonging, the place of inclusion and security. Nehemiah shakes out the pockets of his robe, as a simple visual aid – 'in this way may God shake out of his house and possessions every man that does not keep his promise' (v. 13).

We cannot escape the application of a passage of Scripture like this for our own day. Each of us will need to reflect on what it will mean for us, with our varied economic and cultural and social backgrounds, and the varied Christian communities to which we belong. But let me draw one or two conclusions.

Firstly, equality and generosity arise from basic theological foundations. In 2 Corinthians Paul devotes two chapters to the question of the offering for the needs of hard-pressed Christians in Jerusalem. It was not just to meet needs, it was also seen, by Paul, as an expression of solidarity between Jewish and Gentile Christians. Practical financial help would be a clear signal of the unity of believers from different cultural backgrounds. Paul even called it 'the privilege of sharing in this service to the saints' (8:4). Unselfishness was the mark of true fellowship, expressed across national and cultural boundaries.

The early church, empowered by the Spirit, preached the love of God in Christ, in the context of a community committed to demonstrate that love. If you ask, 'What were the characteristics of the early churches?' They certainly had their problems, but there was no sterile debate about evangelism and social action. The gospel found expression in powerful preaching, fruitful evangelism, extraordinary generosity to those in need, and a deeply caring Christian community.

Secondly, if we genuinely lived this way, we would be a powerful witness to a fractured world which is longing to see true community. This is happening. For example, the Peckham Evangelical Churches' Action Network trains thousands of unemployed people; the Bethany Trust works with the homeless in Edinburgh; Victory Outreach has specialized homes in London for drug addicts and prostitutes. Many of London's black churches are doing a fantastic job with night shelters for the homeless, Sunday meals for people living alone, English classes, counselling services and health clinics.

Linked to this, there is the issue not simply of our solidarity within our own Christian community, but also our solidarity with God's people worldwide. What of our global Christian community? To what extent are we genuinely committed to that? Do we respond in terms of practical fellowship and financial support? This is a daily reality for me as I try to help balance limited resources in our work, encouraging those whom God has blessed materially to help those who are struggling. We need to assess who are the equivalent of Jerusalem's powerless as we think about what true community will mean in our world, and we need to work to build strong partnerships worldwide.

The Jubilee 2000 campaign, which calls for debt cancellation, is supported by thousands of Christians. (Here in the UK we receive £75 million a year in debt repayment from the poorest countries of the world.) Some of us will be called to exercise our influence in political circles, addressing the appalling consequences of crude globalization.

As in Nehemiah's day, the kind of communities we build are a reflection of the kind of God we believe in and that communicates. If on the one hand we declare we are the reconciled people of God, and yet at the same time we fail to display a community of generosity and equality, we are giving conflicting messages. True community arises from the heart of the gospel. It will be a radical alternative to the social alienation and isolation of our own culture.

It is interesting to note that Luke records at the end of Acts 2, 'The Lord added daily to their number' (v. 47). What kind of community was it to which the Lord added people? 'They were praising God and finding favour with all the people.' Just as it was deeply attractive then, this kind of community would be very magnetic in our society now. It's exactly the kind of community our world needs to see.

3. Knowing God's Protection
Nehemiah 4 & 6

During my first experience of sailing, off the Island of Mull, the weather suddenly changed and I was forced to learn to tack. The zig-zag motion may seem slow, but it enables you to use the winds that are against you to make headway. Your journey forward in the Christian life is going to be contested all the way, but by God's grace, those *very* forces of opposition can be used by God to help you make progress.

When Paul was writing to the Thessalonians, he explained that, because of the pressures they were facing, he would send Timothy along to encourage them. Why? 'So that no one would be unsettled by these trials. You know quite well that you were destined for them. In fact, when we were with you we kept telling you that we would be persecuted. And it turned out that way, as you well know' (1 Thess. 3:3).

'You are destined for trials,' Paul says. Calvin's comment on this verse was that it was almost as if Paul was saying, 'You are Christians on this condition': you will face trials. The early Christians knew this. Luke's story in the book of Acts is often seen as an account of two movements: the movement of the Holy Spirit in establishing the church, and the movement of the powers of darkness which oppose that. And so it is today. Anyone involved in the work of God will find themselves under ceaseless pressure to give up. They will confront opposition from all kinds of sources, from outside and inside the Christian community.

It's as well to be honest about this. There is a danger of a form of triumphalism that suggests that Christians should always be riding high on a success-oriented spirituality. The Christian life, in these terms, is one of perpetual positive self-fulfilment. If that is your model of the Christian life, then as soon as you encounter struggles, you either become disillusioned, feeling God has let you down; or you become despairing, feeling that you have failed and have let God down – there must be something wrong with your faith if progress is so demanding.

Anyone seeking to fulfil God's purposes, to run the race to which He has called them, will find themselves confronting one hurdle after another. Difficulties are not a punishment, they are an affirmation and they are to be expected. When we become Christians we undergo a radical change of allegiance. We are taken out of one kingdom – the kingdom of darkness, and transferred into the kingdom of God's dear Son. Neutrality is impossible. If now we are in God's kingdom, living by God's values, we will inevitably be in conflict with a world which is hostile to God.

It would be easy to become paranoid with fear if this was our only perspective of the journey ahead. And so Jesus balances realism with assurance when He says to us in John 16:33, 'In the world you will have trouble.' That's the reality. There's no avoiding that kind of confrontation. 'But take heart. I have overcome the world.' He assures us that in this struggle we will enjoy God's protection. The opposition, however determined and hostile, ultimately have no other expectation than final defeat. 'I have overcome the world.'

The book of Nehemiah begins with a man and a people devoted to a God-given task. They see it as an absolute priority, and carry it out with a determined faithfulness. So, it is no surprise that the story should soon include an account of the relentless opposition they faced. God's work is *always* resisted. In Nehemiah's case, the opposition came at both the personal and the community level. Chapters 4 and 6 identify not only the various forms of attack, but also the specific responses of Nehemiah and the people in countering them.

1) Hostility from God's enemies (4:1–9)

Nehemiah's opponents have already been introduced in chapter 2. They were 'very much disturbed' (v. 10), and seemed to be amused that Nehemiah should be attempting to rebuild the walls (v. 19). But now, as the teams of workers are organized and motivated, and the walls are beginning to rise, the opponents view the matter more seriously. Sanballat is described as 'angry and greatly incensed' (4:1).

There were several reasons why opposition was surfacing. Personal ambition and jealousy were doubtless part of it, but one obvious reason was to do with economic power. One of the major trade routes of the day passed through Jerusalem, and a restored city would mean the loss of economic supremacy for Sanballat, the Samarian governor. He did not want to see Jerusalem become strong again, so he and his allies were determined to put a stop to the reconstruction programme. They started with ridicule. 'What does this bunch of poor feeble Jews think they are doing? Do they think they can build the wall in a day if they offer enough sacrifices? Look at those charred stones they are pulling out of the rubbish and using again!' (v. 2, *New Living Bible*)

This was the beginning of a sustained propaganda campaign, and the fact that Sanballat spoke 'in the presence of his associates and his army' (v. 2), suggests that he was addressing them, as much as the Jews, building his own support base of opposition. The audience would get the message: these were miserable Jews, good for nothing, incapable of turning this heap of rubble into any kind of lasting fortress. The crowd would have loved it – you can hear the sniggers and the taunts. One of Sanballat's close allies, Tobiah, adds to the ridicule: 'That stone wall would collapse if even a fox walked along the top of it' (v. 3).

His sick joke was meant to imply that the opposition hardly needed to lift a finger. Foxes usually lived in ruins, and it only needed one of Jerusalem's foxes to trip lightly across the newly constructed wall to do the job for them. Archaeological research has indicated that Nehemiah's walls were up to 9 feet thick, so it was a foolish thing to say, but the opposition was resorting to psychological warfare in this early stage of their attack. This kind of ridicule impacts people differently. When Jeremiah faced this kind of mockery he felt it keenly. And for God's people building the wall, it was sure to have taken its toll. They were facing a colossal task with limited resources, taking on a project which already had a history of failure, and ridicule wouldn't have been easy.

Mockery, hostility and contempt towards the Christian faith are common in many parts of the world and are likely to increase here in the West – if we are faithful in proclaiming the exclusive claims of Jesus Christ. It might be the gentle mockery of people in the family or in the office, it might be jokes about our Christian lifestyle, or it might be direct hostility by those who object to our Christian commitments and Christian values. Nehemiah's response to the sarcastic ridicule is recorded in verses 4 and 5, to which we will return in a moment. But the people pressed ahead with the work. 'We rebuilt the wall till all of it reached half its height. For the people worked with all their heart' (v. 6). And at the point when the people saw the progress, the opposition gained momentum. The enemies 'plotted together to come and fight against Jerusalem and stir up trouble against it' (v. 8).

Hostility was brewing and Nehemiah introduces the opponents in v. 7:

- Sanballat, who had a Babylonian name and was Governor of Samaria, was in the north.
- Tobiah, who had a Hebrew name, probably ruled over the Ammonite territory to the east.
- The Arabs were Judah's southern neighbour.
- The Ashdodites were in the west.

They were completely surrounded by the four neighbouring provinces of the Persian empire. And this unholy alliance, united in its opposition to the people of God, encircled Jerusalem and intensified its threats. Whether or not they would have carried out their intention is debated, but the hostile threat had to be taken seriously.

Some of my colleagues working in Jerusalem recently set up a stand in the main University Forum in the Hebrew University of Jerusalem to display and give out free literature, New Testaments, and copies of the *Jesus* video. They were quite nervous about going public and they received a mixed reaction. Some were fascinated and were very open, others were furious and offended, tearing up their literature, and one man decided to vent his anger for four hours. Now isn't that courageous of these young believers, who were determined to proclaim the name of Jesus despite that hostility?

It must have been tough for the people on the wall, in Nehemiah 4, to be true to their calling despite what was being said and despite the armies beginning to range around the city. Whilst the external attack gathered momentum, something was happening amongst God's people which represented another form of pressure for Nehemiah.

2) Defeatism amongst God's people (4:10–12)

There were three problems: Discouragement (v. 10), intimidation (v. 11) and pessimism (v. 12).

Discouragement was understandable. As verse 6 indicated, they were half way through the project and that's always the most difficult moment. It's similar to climbing a mountain. After the initial burst of energetic enthusiasm, you see rise after rise in the distance, with no sight of the summit, and you soon draw the conclusion that you stand no chance of making it. The people on the wall were overwhelmed with tiredness (the word for strength 'giving out' means stumble, totter). They were carting huge rocks day and night and were completely disheartened by the mounds of rubble which still lay all around them. Are you close to throwing in the towel? It's a very common experience. A high proportion of missionaries brought home for health reasons and emotional exhaustion today face similar occupational hazards to David Livingstone 120 years ago. 'Livingstone was often deeply depressed. Between 1853 and 1856 he suffered 30 attacks of malaria, and his wife died of the disease on the Zambezi river when she was forty. By the time Stanley found him, he was worn out mentally and physically, his supplies had been stolen and he had no medicines. He was almost at the end of the road.'

We can't escape such feelings of physical, emotional and spiritual exhaustion. (One of my colleagues said, 'The only thing holding me together is perpetual motion!' In other words, if she stopped, she would collapse.) Anyone committed to making a difference for the Lord in their personal witness, whether in evangelism or in living by Christian values and standards, will find they frequently feel the exhaustion of fighting on the front. Can you imagine how Nehemiah must have felt? Ridicule and threats were within earshot, the possibility of guerrilla tactics and terrorist incursions whilst the wall was incomplete was great, and the despairing complaints of his own team were inside the wall.

Sometimes this kind of discouragement is one of the greatest weapons of the enemy. Jim Packer talks about the problem of 'attitudinal rubble' in the church:

> Pastors and spiritual leaders today, whose concerns extend beyond maintenance to mission, and who seek a genuine extending of God's kingdom, find themselves faced again and again with what has to be classed as attitudinal rubble – laziness, unbelief, procrastination, cynicism, self-absorption, in-fighting and fence-sitting among the Lord's people, and many similar factors that hinder and obstruct spiritual advance.

Intimidation grew. The people of Judah were taken in by the whispering campaign of the enemy, injecting a continuous stream of propaganda. 'Before they know it or see us, we will be right there among them and will kill them and put an end to their work' (v. 11). This was gnawing away at their morale and steadily undermining their confidence. It is the kind of thing Satan exploits in our lives too, whispering in our ears, accusing us, exploiting our weaknesses, predicting failure, lying about God's promises. And facing determined opposition is exhausting. We can easily become paralysed in the face of intimidation.

Pessimism began to surface. The prophets of doom, who are found in every community of God's people, were living in the nearby villages, undoubtedly under threat themselves, and they began to urge the people in Jerusalem to abandon the sinking ship before it was too late. It's a doomed city, they said. 'Wherever you go they will attack us' (v. 12). Give up now. You'll never make it. Have you ever heard that before in your church? With friends like these I am sure Nehemiah thought, 'Who needs enemies outside the wall?'

Alongside the growing pressure on Nehemiah and the community we see their responses to the opposition. Seven times in chapters 4 and 6, Nehemiah makes a journal note that reflects his dependence on God. He also records the practical action taken by the people. There are two responses which we need to apply to our own lives, as we face hostility from enemies and defeatism amongst God's people.

a) Remember the Lord

The text shows how Nehemiah constantly returned to the God of heaven, the One who had called him to the task.

1) *He remembered God's justice* (vv. 4, 5). Nehemiah's prayer has provoked some disagreement amongst commentators. Is it a model of how we should respond to enemies? Doesn't it introduce a jarring note in Christian minds? Surely Jesus taught us a different way in the Sermon on the Mount (Mt. 5:43–48)? Surely Paul urged us to bless, not to curse, those who persecute us? That's true. At the same time, we should recall that such prayers in the Old Testament reflect an attitude of concern for God's honour. When the enemies oppose the workers on the wall, they are, in reality, opposing the work of God. It is His name which is being mocked, His cause which is being slandered. What do we make of this kind of prayer?

The imprecatory psalms (which include a spoken curse) and the prayers of Nehemiah and Jeremiah are expressions of anger at the fact that men are shaking their little fists at God, expressions of longing that God would vindicate Himself. They are concerned for God's honour. Nehemiah saw that

God's name was being mocked and His cause being slandered. So when we see these expressions of anger, we understand they are appealing for God to be true to His name and nature, to act justly and demonstrate His universal authority.

When Jesus faced enemies who insulted him, as Peter wrote, 'he entrusted himself to him who judges justly ...' (1 Pet. 2:23). Don't always fight back, entrust yourself to Him who judges justly. When we are facing the hostility of God's enemies today, we can be sure of God's justice being ultimately fulfilled. In Psalm 73, the psalmist couldn't understand why God had allowed the apparent success of the 'fat cats' who opposed Him, 'until I entered the sanctuary of God; then I understood their final destiny' (v. 17). When he came into God's presence, and realized that God is the Judge of all, he remembered what would happen in the end. So, whatever the opposition we face, we can be absolutely sure that God's justice will be done, His purposes will not be defeated.

2) *He remembered God's protection* (v. 9). 'But we prayed to our God and posted a guard day and night to meet this threat.' Knowing that this was God's work, Nehemiah clearly sustained his praying, and encouraged the people to join him. 'We prayed to our God', that He would protect them from their enemies. And we shouldn't underestimate the importance of praying for protection in our own lives and Christian ministries. I am enormously grateful for the team of committed people who pray for me and for my family regularly.

I recently read a report from Central Africa about a young pastor and his family who asked if they could pray before they died, when Tutsi soldiers broke into their house. After praying, the family slowly stood up and saw that the soldiers were gone; not only out of their house but away from their village as well. Later, one of the Tutsi soldiers who had been there, came into a church and gave this testimony,:

> You see, I was there when we broke into your house. I was the one who had your children lined up in my gun

sight as you kneeled and prayed … when suddenly a wall of fire, fierce and ferocious, jumped up and surrounded you. We couldn't even see beyond the flames. Due to the intense heat we knew the house would burn down so we fled. When we went outside and saw the house consumed by fire yet not destroyed, we fled the village as well. Later I realized this was a fire sent by God. If this is how your God responds, I want to know Him too. I am tired of the fighting and killing. This is why I came tonight.

I could also recount stories of colleagues and friends of mine who have lost their lives for the cause of Christ in the last few years. We Christians carry no immunity from suffering or martyrdom, and we cannot fathom the mysteries of why God might appear to intervene on some occasions and not others. We have to trust His good purposes. The list of heroes of faith in Hebrews 11 demonstrates that some were snatched from the jaws of death, and some were sawn in two; both equally trusted God and this is all part of the mystery. We are encouraged to seek God's protection, and not take it for granted.

3) *He remembered God's power* (vv. 14, 15). 'After I looked things over, I stood up and said to the nobles, the officials and the rest of the people, "Don't be afraid of them. Remember the Lord, who is great and awesome, and fight for your brothers, your sons and your daughters, your wives and your homes."' He uses the language of his prayer in chapter 1, to encourage the people to refocus on the God of power, the Sovereign Lord who achieves His purposes. That kind of thoughtful reflection puts the opposition into perspective.

For the Christian, calling to mind what God has achieved through Christ provides the perspective for our spiritual warfare. Colossians 2 gives us a wonderful mandate for our praying, reminding us that the certainty of victory in the warfare is absolutely guaranteed because of Jesus and His cross. 'And having disarmed the powers and authorities, he made a public spectacle of them, triumphing over them by the cross' (2:15). The picture is of evil spirit powers – 'terrorists from hell' – stripped of their weapons. On the cross Jesus defeated every evil power, He triumphed over His enemies, set captives free and destroyed the captor. We are not free from our struggle with hostile forces, but we know the final outcome of the battle is absolutely sure. What Jesus did on the cross means that the opposition forces face final ruin.

It's rather like watching a video replay of a match you know your team won. You are tempted to believe the opposition will score and win but you already know the result.

We know the outcome of our struggle. We are to keep alert to Satan's devices, but most of all we are to keep our eyes on Jesus, on the risen Lord who has defeated death. Satan, the principalities and powers and death itself have no other expectation than final ruin. And the focus of that victory in our lives, and in our universe, is the Lord Jesus, crucified in weakness. We have won. We are not fighting *for* a position of victory but *from* a position of victory (F.F. Bruce).

4) *He remembered God's commitment*: 'Wherever you hear the sound of the trumpet, join us there. Our God will fight for us!' (v. 20) In the midst of the pressure, this verse suggests that now the people have a new purposefulness about them, a new courage. This is God's work, and as verse 20 suggests, He is committed to see it through. He is guaranteeing the outcome. Our God will fight for us!

Alongside these four calls to remember the Lord, we should note the second feature of their response: man's action.

b) *They posted a guard* (v. 9)

Taking various precautions and concentrating their defences, the people strengthened their sense of solidarity in fighting for one another; they developed an attitude of war alert and were constantly vigilant. They kept their clothes on rather than wearing pyjamas! They were ready, watching the exposed places, verse 13, those points of weakness which needed special care.

And as we pray for God's protection, Paul encourages us in Ephesians 6 to 'put on the whole armour of God, so that you can take your stand against the devil's schemes'. This is no game: we need to be equipped, to be ready to use the weaponry, which God has provided for us. I am sure we need to trust God's Word and Spirit more in our lives, keeping alert to Satan's devices and standing alongside one another in the battle, praying in the Spirit, 'Be strong in the Lord and in his mighty power' (6:10).

They posted a guard, but still faced three remaining challenges.

3) Distraction from the task (6:1–4)

By 6:1 the wall was all but completed, and we might think that the opposition would realize it had lost the day. But no! The opposition was there at the beginning in chapter 1, it was there half way through chapter 4, it is here in chapter 6. Opposition to God's work is not only inevitable, it is sustained. We will face it until we get to heaven. The enemies were active when the wall began, when the wall was half completed, and as the wall was nearing its completion. But the attacks now took a more subtle and more difficult turn. They were concentrated around Nehemiah himself.

The first, couched initially in diplomatic terms, was an attempt by Sanballat to eliminate Nehemiah. A messenger arrived suggesting it was time for negotiations. 'Come, let us meet together in one of the villages on the plain of Ono.' Let's sit down and talk it through. This was nothing more than a subtle piece of smooth talking as Nehemiah notes: 'They were scheming to harm me' (v. 2). The work was in its final stages and Nehemiah knew that, apart from the wasted time in travelling to the plain of Ono, the greater danger was the obvious personal threat to which he would become vulnerable if he left his friends.

So, what was his response to this form of opposition? It was clear and unequivocal: 'I am carrying on a great project and cannot go down. Why should I stop work while I leave it and go down to you?' (v. 3). Four times they sent the same message (v. 4): don't be small-minded Nehemiah, be reasonable. But he refused to budge. The overriding priority was the work God had called him to do, and he would not be distracted or diverted from it.

That's a common form of attack for us Christians, isn't it? Satan often whispers, 'You've done OK, you can relax a little. There's no need to be a fanatic.' We are frequently tempted by diversions and distractions of all kinds. Sometimes, they can be entirely legitimate things, which mean that the priority calling is neglected. It happened in the early church. Luke records in Acts 6 how the apostles were confronted with a problem within the Christian community that not only had the potential to cause division, but equally seriously, was in danger of diverting them from their primary tasks. Wisely they called others to deal with the immediate practical problem, so that they could give their attention to the ministry of the Word and prayer.

We need to learn from Nehemiah's response. In the face of distraction, remember your calling.

4) A challenge to his reputation (6:5–9)

Having failed to pull Nehemiah away from the work, Sanballat decided to turn the screw a little more. On the fifth attempt, Sanballat's aide arrived with an open letter. Let me paraphrase: 'Rumour has it that you are actually planning an armed revolt against the Persian King and would like the throne for yourself. Would you care to comment?' (v. 6).

Being unsealed, of course, it was the equivalent to a letter to *The Times*. It was a slanderous accusation, and it was now out in the open, outside Nehemiah's control. As we've seen, the king had earlier put a stop to the rebuilding programme that had been attempted (Ezra 4), precisely because of such an accusation. So Sanballat was adopting a smear campaign to blackmail Nehemiah. It is what in political jargon is called 'opposition research'. You try to manufacture something that will smear the character, some mud that might stick. The victim's only defence is a clear conscience. Nehemiah could reply with integrity, 'Nothing like what you are saying is happening; you are just making it up out of your head' (v. 8).

The ability to live our lives with integrity is the only protection against that kind of slander. It is impressive that when Paul was criticized, he could frequently appeal to both fellow Christians and to God himself as a witness to how he had lived. 'You are witnesses and so is God of how holy, righteous and blameless we were among you who believed' (1 Thess. 2:5, 10).

Nehemiah and Paul knew that the best response, when their motives or character were attacked, was to keep a clear conscience. It will be painful when people say things about you that are not true. And for this we need the Lord's help: 'Now strengthen my hands' (v. 9). Ignore the gossip; trust your cause to God.

5) The temptation to compromise (6:10–14)

The final attack was more subtle still. Shemaiah informed Nehemiah that he was on a hit list: 'By night they are coming to kill you' (v. 10). So he urged him to take refuge inside the temple. Coming from someone who professed to be a prophet, the proposal had a religious veneer.

But Nehemiah was just as uncompromising as ever. There was no way in which he would be seen to run. He would lose credibility as a leader if he tried to hide from threatened attack. There was also no way in which he would enter the temple (v. 12). He was a layman, not a priest, and he knew that even to enter the temple, under the ruse of saving his life, would only end in disaster. It was not permitted in the Scriptures. Because he knew God's word, he could test the prophecy. 'I realised that God had not sent him, but that he had prophesied against me because Tobiah and Sanballat had hired him. He had been hired to intimidate me so that I would commit a sin by doing this, and then they would give me a bad name to discredit me' (v. 12).

His reponse to this attack: he was determined to live by

the truth. Calvin says, 'It is an artifice of Satan to seek some misconduct on the part of ministers which may tend to the dishonour of the gospel.' It is not only Christian leaders but all of us who face such pressure. We are constantly tempted to compromise. It might be to compromise on the essential truth of the Christian faith. It might be the temptation to compromise on its moral demands on our lives. It might be the temptation to compromise sexually, or financially, or to misuse power. Our protection will be to live by the Truth, for our lives to be shaped by that Word, and for the Spirit to empower us to be consistent in living by its standards.

Let me conclude: it is well said that if we in the West compromised less, we would undoubtedly suffer more. As Dietrich Bonhoeffer wrote in *The Cost of Discipleship* before he was executed by the direct orders of Himmler, shortly before the Allies liberated the concentration camp in which he was being held, 'Suffering is the badge of the true Christian.' There is no escaping it if we name the name of Christ.

But the story of these two chapters highlights the twin themes with which we began – the wind against the boat and the progress the boat makes.

The winds kept on blowing for Nehemiah. In chapter 6 the account is punctuated three times by his diary note: 'They were all trying to frighten us' (v. 9); 'the prophets who have been trying to intimidate me' (v. 14). And even after the wall was completed, the slander and intimidation kept coming: 'And Tobiah sent letters to intimidate me' (v. 19). This is what Alec Motyer once called 'the constant dripping of Satanic acid'. Deceit, espionage, slander – something coming through the post every day to eat away at his morale and to distract him from the job God had called him to do.

But those winds had the opposite effect. They enabled Nehemiah and the people to finish the task because they focused their attention on what really mattered. They trusted God more wholeheartedly. It's when we're in this situation that God teaches us to hold Him fast. The winds against us are the very things which help us to complete the journey. 'When all our enemies heard about this, all the surrounding nations

were afraid and lost their self-confidence, because they realised that this work had been done with the help of our God'
(6:16).

We all need to have the assurance that it is the Sovereign
Lord, the God of heaven, who will fulfil His purposes with us
and through us. Just as I learned the lesson tacking up the
Sound of Mull, so God would say to hard-pressed Christians
that His purpose is not to bypass difficulties in our lives, but to
transform them, so that we say this work has been done with
the help of our God.

4. Responding to God's Word
Nehemiah 8–10

'I believe in a bit of everything – God, the supernatural, ghosts, superstitions, UFOs. I like to keep my options open.'

These words, of the former England cricket captain Mike Gatting, sum up the extraordinary sense of confusion which characterizes people's beliefs today. They illustrate that 'when people stop believing in the truth, they don't believe in nothing, they believe in anything' (G.K. Chesterton).

In the recent BBC1 series entitled 'The Soul of Britain', in which Michael Buerk attempted to assess the religious mood of this country, he concluded: 'Buddhism is growing as the statistics show a marked turn from notions of religion to the ideas of spirituality. We seem to be turning away from traditional forms of faith, associated with a dogmatic, theological approach. Instead, people are looking for a more experiential faith across the global spectrum.'

Nowadays, words like 'doctrine' or 'dogma' go along with 'bigot' as words of disapproval. As someone once wittily remarked, 'These days, any stigma is good enough to beat a dogma with.' Our culture has undergone a radical transformation when it comes to the issue of truth. There are now three main philosophies:

1) *Traditional* – Truth is objective, independent of the mind of the knower, and it's there to be discovered.

2) *Relativism* – Truth 'as each person sees it'. It's one thing to you, it's another thing to me.
3) *Post-modern* – Truth is not there to be discovered, but it is for 'each of us to create for ourselves'. The truth is what I make it.

This last attitude is much more common than we might imagine. Truth is subjective. It's true because I like it; it's true if it helps me. Truth is a commodity to be moulded to serve my ends. When a Christian student who was having some struggles went to a university counsellor, she was advised to go and sleep with her boyfriend. 'No, I'm a Christian, that's wrong,' she replied. To which the student counsellor responded, 'If it's functionally helpful, then it's legitimate.'

This is truth that is shaped according to the patterns of our own desires and convenience and which makes no demands on us. If it helps then it must be true. The inevitable result of this view is that ultimately people – and societies – lose their bearings, becoming confused and morally bewildered.

A few years ago, a Gallup poll indicated that most people believe that Britain is in severe moral decline. The *Sunday Times* editorial on the subject talked of 'a nation ill at ease with its conscience', where 'only one in five believes there is a broadly agreed set of moral standards'. It would be easy for Christians to respond with a degree of 'I-told-you-so' smugness, or with much wringing of hands. But we must feel our responsibility for the situation and, like Nehemiah, we should resist the temptation to stand apart, indifferent to the moral and spiritual decline, and see that God has called us to serve Him at a unique moment. If Michael Buerk's analysis is true, if there is an underlying longing for some form of spirituality, then this is also a hopeful moment. We do have the opportunity, as God's people, to try and respond to their bewilderment and uncertainty.

In Nehemiah 8 we encounter an extraordinary turning point in the reconstruction of the national life of God's people. The rebuilding of the wall was finished, but that represented only the beginning. What really mattered was the shaping of the people, the reordering of their community life according to a solid constitution, with a proper foundation for their future as the distinct people of a Holy God. 'When the seventh month came and the Israelites had settled in their towns, all the people assembled as one man in the square before the Water Gate. They told Ezra the scribe to bring out the Book of the Law of Moses, which the Lord had commanded for Israel' (8:1). They were about to embark on a massive re-education programme, which was to form the foundation for their spiritual, moral, social and economic life. As Derek Kidner says, they were to become 'the people of the Book'.

Would it be an exaggeration to say that today, as God's people, we too need to engage in a massive programme of re-education? If God's Word were more fully a part of our lives, transforming us in our families, our worship, our professional life, our social and moral behaviour, we would be living as people of hope in a relatively despairing society. Those who comment on the state of the church today suggest that we too have drifted. Writing 35 years ago in his book, *God Has Spoken*, Jim Packer said:

> At no time perhaps since the Reformation have protestant Christians, as a body, been so unsure, so tentative and confused as to what they should believe and do. Certainty about the great issues of Christian faith and conduct is lacking all along the line. The outside observer sees us staggering on from gimmick to gimmick and stunt to stunt like so many drunks in a fog, not knowing at all where we are or which way we should be going. Preaching is hazy; heads are muddled; hearts fret; doubts drain our strength; uncertainty paralyses action.

Since Dr Packer wrote those words, maybe there are signs of a turning of the tide. Christian people are longing to live lives that reflect God's standards, to do more than accumulate scriptural knowledge and to experience the transforming power of the Word to make us different. But for sure, there is a long way to go.

1) The foundation of God's Word

Chapter 8:1 introduces us to something with which we're familiar – a 7-day Bible conference! It marks the close of the narrative we have been following thus far and introduces us to a new section of the book with three vital chapters all about the spiritual restoration of God's people, under the shared leadership of Ezra and Nehemiah.

It's possible that this section of Nehemiah once belonged between Ezra 8 and 9. But its place here, at the centre of Nehemiah's account, is theologically significant. The building of the walls might be over, but the true foundation for the restored community will be God's Word. Nehemiah knew how central and strategic this would be, and so he ensures that Ezra the scholar-teacher now comes to the fore.

I suggest three features of the text which demonstrate that Ezra and Nehemiah saw the Word as the foundation for all that was to follow:

a) Its centrality

The seventh month for God's people was a month of great religious festivity, and their first act was to call for the Book. There was a grassroots desire that the Law should be read: 'All the people assembled before the Water Gate. They told Ezra the scribe to bring out the Book of the Law of Moses, which the Lord had commanded for Israel' (8:1).

And the Law commanded the attention of everyone: 'all the people listened attentively' (v. 3); 'on the second day of the month, the heads of the families gathered around Ezra to give attention to the words of the Law' (v. 13); 'day after day, from the first day to the last, Ezra read from the Book of the Law of God' (v. 18). It retained this central place right through to the end of the month: 'They stood where they were and they read from the Book of the Law of the Lord their God for a quarter of the day' (9:3). At the end of chapter 12, we have the account of the joyful processions as the walls are dedicated, and Nehemiah records, 'On that day the Book of Moses was read aloud in the hearing of the people' (13:1).

The Word of God represented the foundation articles, the

new constitution for the people of God. They had come back from exile to Jerusalem and now, placed at the very centre of their life, was what God had to say to them. It defined their identity.

In the Central Asian Republics, children now have to learn huge chunks of the Koran in their Islamic schools. Stalin might have closed 26,000 mosques, but new investment is ensuring that the book is being read as a foundation for Islam in the battle of ideologies in this post-Soviet world. What about the place of *The* Book, God's Word, in our own society? We may now be in a post-Christian culture, but one of our challenges is to call people back to Scripture. When Theodore Roosevelt wrote about Abraham Lincoln, he described his core commitments: 'Lincoln built up his entire reading upon his study of the Bible. He mastered it and became a man who knew the Book and instinctively put into practice what he had been taught therein.'

Well, that was the desire of the Jews on that day in Nehemiah 8:1. For a nation seeking its identity and shaping its programme of restoration, the Word of God mattered. It was central. There is even something symbolic in the fact that it was not read in the temple: 'He read it aloud from daybreak till noon as he faced the square before the Water Gate' (v. 3). It was read 'at one of the centres of city life, the kind of place where God's wisdom pleads most urgently to be heard. The law itself insisted that its voice must not be confined to the sanctuary but heard in the house and the street' (D. Kidner). This is stressed in Deuteronomy 6:7, 'Impress them on your children. Talk about them when you sit at home and when you walk along the road.' Make the truth of God's Word central to the whole of life.

b) Its authority

'They told Ezra the scribe to bring out the Book of the Law of Moses, which the Lord had commanded for Israel' (v. 1). Its human authorship is acknowledged on several occasions – the reading was from the books of Moses, but its divine authority is emphasized – the law of God, the revelation, was given by Him. The instruction came from God Himself for their well-being. Without this sense of divine authority it would simply be the veneration of a book. We are sometimes accused at Keswick of just venerating an ancient text. It is vital we realize that the Word has authority because of the God who speaks that Word.

There is a powerful verse in 1 Thessalonians 2:13, where Paul describes the way in which the believers received the gospel, which can transform our attitude to the Bible. 'We thank God continually because, when you received the word of God, which you heard from us, you accepted it not as the word of men, but as it actually is, the word of God which is at work in you who believe.'

Note four implications:

Its authority: it is 'the Word *of God*'. Paul writes emphatically that the message of the apostles is authoritative because it originates with God Himself. In our pluralistic culture, when we are trying to proclaim the gospel, or preach God's Word, we need to do it with great sensitivity. We are often asked, 'You Christians, what right have you to talk about Jesus as the only way?' And what we have to do, with humility, is to take a step back and acknowledge in our own hearts that this is the Word of God. We are often tempted, even as evangelicals, to lose our nerve in affirming Jesus as the only way and affirming the Scriptures as the Word of God.

Its power: 'which is at work in you who believe'. It is powerful precisely because it is God's Word. We shouldn't drive a wedge between the written Word and the living God who speaks that Word. By God's Spirit it is powerful, life-giving, life-transforming. You could translate that verse, 'It goes on working in those who go on believing.'

Its reception: Paul thanks God that the Thessalonian believers 'accepted it' as God's Word. He uses two words in v. 13 – they 'received' the Word, that means they heard it, but they also 'accepted' it, they welcomed it in as a friend, it became part of them, continuing its work in their lives.

Its impact: in 1 Thessalonians 9 he describes the way in which they turned from idols to serve the living God. Then, 'the Lord's message rang out from you… your faith in God has become known everywhere' (1 Thess. 1:8).

God's transforming Word is not simply propositional truth, distant, cold and remote, but a dynamic Word that, by the power of the Spirit, turns us round to serve God, and shapes the way we live.

c) Its accessibility

If God's Word was to be the foundation for families' day to day living, society and relationships, then it had to be clear and accessible to everyone. There are two features to notice:

Everyone was present: 'All the people assembled as one man' (8:1); Ezra read before the assembly, verse 2, 'which was made up of men and women and all who were able to understand' (children); then verse 5, 'all the people could see him' (no TV monitors but a wooden tower); verse 9, 'they were all weeping'; verse 13, 'the heads of all the families'. So every attempt was made to ensure that everyone was present. Verse 4 demonstrates that Ezra got a team together to help with the reading. It was not just for priests or Levites, the religious professionals, but in the city centre rather than the temple, and for all, young and old.

It was not only vital that everyone was present, but also that:

Everyone understood: the account shows us the stress placed on understanding for men, women and children. The content of the law had to be clear, 'giving the meaning so that the people could understand what was being read' (v. 8). The reason for the people's response is obvious, 'because they now understood the words that had been made known to them' (v. 12).

It's possible that the list of Levites in verses 7 and 8 were involved in translation into the language that the people understood – Aramaic and various dialects. Or, it's possible that they moved through the crowds holding small-group Bible studies, explaining what the text meant. What comes across clearly is the need to make the Book accessible to everybody, whether in the manner in which Ezra used his team, or the location he chose for the reading, or the tower that was constructed, or the groups of translators and expositors and Bible study group leaders that he employed.

We need hardly make the point of application about the foundation of God's Word. We need to work creatively today to ensure that everyone is exposed to the truth of Scripture through sustaining clear, relevant, applied Bible exposition, but also through the many interactive approaches, through small groups, through the new media which are now available to us.

2) The hunger of God's people

There are three themes to point out.

a) *Their expectancy*

They were eager to hear the Word. They wanted the Law and the Lord to speak to them. They took the initiative, calling on Ezra to bring out the Book.

The same sense of eagerness and expectancy is expressed in verse 3: 'all the people listened attentively'; verse 5, as the people 'stood up' when the Book was opened; and verse 13: 'everyone gathered to give attention to the words of the Law'. It reminds us of Luke's comment in Acts 17:11, when he describes the Bereans, who 'received the message with great eagerness and examined the Scriptures every day to see if what Paul said was true'. It also reminds us that there is little to be gained from reading the Bible without such expectancy. Jesus' own ministry was frustrated when there was no expectancy on the part of some of his hearers – He began to teach in the synagogue and He was met with cynicism and incredulity. Expectant faith is the soil in which God's Word will bear fruit in our lives.

b) *Their commitment*

A further sign of their spiritual hunger was their seriousness. They were ready to cope with all kinds of inconvenience in order to hear this Word. I have sometimes been in Eastern European countries where, after preaching for two hours, the congregation wonders why you've stopped! Here the

Water Gate congregation stood from daybreak to noon (v. 3) – for at least five hours, without a coffee-break in sight – because they longed to hear and understand what God had to say to them.

Again, we have to conclude that this kind of response of commitment to God's Word and eagerness was to do with God's Spirit. There are many things we need to do to make God's Word accessible and understandable, but more than anything else, we need the Holy Spirit to reverse the tide, to create within us and within our churches and even in our society and amongst our politicians, a hunger for what God has to say to us.

There is evidence of a decline in personal and group Bible study. We ought to pray much, much more for this kind of expectancy and seriousness if we are going to reverse this decline. A Bible Society survey showed that almost 40 per cent of churchgoers read the Bible at home only once a year or less. It is a paradox when we think of the availability of Scripture. Our congregations will never mature, our impact on society will never be significant, and our hopes of revival will remain distant, until we develop a stronger desire to read, understand and apply this living dynamic Word to our lives. And this is what Keswick weeks are all about, not just reading for its own sake, but to bring us into God's presence, transform our lives and impact the society where God has placed us.

c) Their reverence

'Ezra praised the Lord, the great God; and all the people lifted their hands and responded, Amen! Amen! Then they bowed down and worshipped the Lord with their faces to the ground' (v. 6).

Today, there is a right sense in which we are concerned to make our church events user-friendly and welcoming. We shouldn't have subcultural barriers stopping people coming in and being part of the Christian community, but along the way we might sometimes have lost a degree of reverence that is appropriate in worship. I am not suggesting we must all adopt the custom of some churches, whereby the congregation stands as the Word of God is carried into the church. But maybe there is something to learn from the attitude of the people in Jerusalem on that day – a longing for God to speak as they lifted up their hands, and self-abasement or reverence and respect, as they bowed with their faces to the ground. Perhaps these too are pre-requisites to understanding God's Word and coming into His presence.

Indeed, the verse is important in reminding us that we don't venerate the Book as such. Its purpose is to bring us into the presence of the author, the Lord, the great God. Luther used to describe Scripture as 'the cradle in which we will find the baby'. Its purpose is not to draw attention to itself, but to introduce us to the person of Jesus. We come to Scripture because it's the way that God will lead us into His presence. Because it's the living Word, because it's dynamic, it will introduce us to the living God and transform us into His likeness.

Jim Packer says in his book, *God Has Spoken*:

> The joy of Bible study is not the fun of collecting esoteric titbits about Gog and Magog, Tubal Cain and Methusalah, Bible numerics and the beast, and so on; nor is it the pleasure, intense for the tidy minded, of analyzing our translated text into preachers' pretty patterns, with neatly numbered headings held together by apt alliterations' artful aid. Rather, it is the deep contentment that comes from communing with the living Lord into whose presence the Bible takes us – a joy which only His own true disciples know.

The next section of the passage introduces us to that dimension – the people experienced God's Word in such a way that it called forth a response at a variety of levels.

3) The implications of God's grace

'For all the people had been weeping as they listened to the words of the Law' (v. 9). Their first hearing of the Law provoked within the people a sense of contrition as they realized that their lives had failed to match up to God's standards. But intriguingly, Ezra and Nehemiah move quickly to set that failure within the wider context of God's purposes for His people. 'This day is sacred to the Lord your God. Do not mourn or weep... Go and enjoy choice food and sweet drinks, and send some to those who have nothing prepared. 'This day is sacred to our Lord. Do not grieve, for the joy of the Lord is your strength' (vv. 9, 10). Their first response should be to accept joyfully all that God has done for them. It was a special day, a day to recall God's grace upon them as His own people.

a) Celebration

This was how they were to respond to God's grace and with the encouragement of the leaders, the people went to celebrate, to eat and drink 'with great joy' (v. 12). After hours of standing, they must have headed off for the party with added zest! Now that they were finally back home in Jerusalem, they had come to realize, from all that had been read, that God's desire was to bless them: 'They now understood the words that had been made known to them' (v. 12). That was the reason why the 'joy of the Lord' was their strength – the word means their 'fortress', their 'stronghold'. It's the awareness that God has good purposes for us, that His Law is for our benefit and that His actions of mercy and grace are for our well-being, our *shalom*. Full appreciation of that generates a deep sense of joy and thanksgiving in our lives. It is the opposite of the anxiety which is so characteristic of our culture.

The note of joy runs on into the next section too. On the second day (v. 13) their Bible study leads them to the discovery of the Feast of Booths, a harvest festival, when they specially remembered deliverance from Egypt and the long march to the Promised Land. So, just as it was written in Leviticus 23, they went out and built their shanty huts. For seven days they were not just celebrating the liberation of God's people from Egypt, but also their own return from exile. 'The whole company that had returned from exile built booths and lived in them. From the days of Joshua son of Nun until that day, the Israelites had not celebrated it like this. And their joy was very great' (v. 17). Notice that it was inclusive: they cared for those who were without resources – another dimension of their community life which demonstrated compassion for those in need.

Believe it or not, joy should be the hallmark of true Christian faith! Of course, how we express it is sometimes to do with our personalities, which God respects; and sometimes to do with our culture, which again God respects. But what have we done to provoke so many people to imagine that the Christian faith is quite the opposite of what is described here? Reverence and joy are not incompatible. Before his conversion, Ernest Gordon, the author of *Miracle on the River Kwai*, thought of Christians as people who extracted the bubbles from the champagne of life. He said 'I would prefer a robust hell to the grey, sunless abode of the faithful.' I know that when people describe the church as deadly boring it is saying as much about them as about the church. But so often there is the missing dimension of celebration. Do you know the story of the young boy who was sitting in a church with his father, looking at various flags hanging from the walls? He asked his father what they were for. 'They're to commemorate the people who died in the services,' he replied. 'Oh,' said the boy, 'Was that the morning or the evening services?'

I like the remark of the German pastor and theologian, Helmut Thielicke, 'Should we not see that lines of laughter about the eyes are just as much marks of faith as are lines of care and seriousness?' The joy of the Lord is our strength – not triumphalism, but the certainty that God has nothing but good purposes for us as His people. That's what came home to them, this inner conviction that would help them to rise above all kinds of challenges, as it does for us.

b) Confession

After the celebrations surrounding the Feast of Booths the people now gather (9:1), fasting and wearing sackcloth and having dust on their heads. Reading the Law leads to confession, which leads to a renewed commitment to keep that Law. It would be true to say that chapter 9, whilst introduced as a confession of sin, is much more a confession of faith. The structure of the prayer demonstrates an oscillation from admission of their failure back to an acknowledgement of God's grace and mercy to them.

It shows us the commitment of the covenant Lord, His persevering steadfast love. There is a statement of God's goodness, then of the people's failure, then of His unfailing mercy:

v. 17   But you are a forgiving God, gracious and compassionate.

v. 19   Because of your great compassion you did not abandon them in the desert.

v. 27   From heaven you heard them, and in your great compassion you gave them deliverers who rescued them from the hand of their enemies.

v. 28   When they cried out to you again, you heard from heaven, and in your compassion you delivered them time after time.

v. 31   But in your great mercy you did not put an end to them or abandon them, for you are a gracious and merciful God. Now therefore, O our God, the great, mighty and awesome God, who keeps his covenant of love, do let all this hardship seem trifling in your eyes.

Notice the 'But' – the wonderful 'But'. Despite the sinfulness, despite the rebellion which had brought them into exile in the first place, God says 'But'. Paul, in Romans 3:21, shows how the 'But' is the turning point of the gospel. 'But now a righteousness from God has been made known. But now through faith in Jesus we are justified freely by his grace through the redemption that came through Christ Jesus.' Aren't you grateful for the 'But now' of the gospel?

As a 14-year-old, I witnessed down on the London Embankment to a crowd of men who had come in off the streets. 'It's OK for you,' one man said, 'but you don't know what I've done. God could never forgive me.' An older and wiser Christian who was with me pointed him to Psalm 103:11–13, 'For as high as the heavens are above the earth, so great is his love for those who fear him; as far as the east is from the west, so far has he removed our transgressions from us. As a father has compassion on his children, so the Lord has compassion on those who fear him.'

Nehemiah's confession of faith in chapter 9 declares that we need not feel the debilitating and demoralizing impact of failure. 'But in your great mercy you did not put an end to them or abandon them, for you are a gracious and merciful God' (v. 31). As we know from the New Testament, Jesus declares to us, by His word and His work, that our sin is forgiven, our guilt is taken away, our pardon is guaranteed. Forgiveness has the liberating effect of lifting the burden. 'If we confess our sins he is faithful and just to forgive us our sins and to cleanse us from all unrighteousness' (1 Jn. 1:9).

Past failures need not hold us back. We sometimes behave as if we have a video of past failure, and even though God assures us it is forgiven and forgotten, we sit there rewinding the video – stop, rewind, play, stop, rewind, play. But our sin is 'covered', as Psalm 51 declares. God's loving purpose for us is that we put down the remote control. We must let go of the past because He has done so, and we learn by His grace to accept the complete forgiveness He has provided in Christ and His cross. That is what the people in this passage recognized, this wonderful confession of faith: *but God* in His mercy has not let go of us.

c) Commitment

The final response naturally follows. Anyone who has experienced this restoring grace of God in their lives will want to commit themselves to live for Him more and more fully. And so, the prayer moves towards a statement of covenant renewal, 'In view of all this, we are making a binding agreement, putting it in writing, and our leaders, our Levites and our priests are affixing their seals to it' (v. 38). They were going to obey God's word. They were 'binding themselves with a curse and an oath to follow the Law of God given through Moses the servant of God and to obey carefully all the commands, regulations, and decrees of the Lord our God' (10:29). They were ready for action. They wanted to live their lives in conformity with God's Word, to demonstrate in their community that they belonged to Him.

That's the significance of the sequence of these chapters: hearing God's word, celebrating God's goodness, knowing God's grace and then obeying God's laws. Truth in action: godliness in working clothes. We are called to *do* the truth, not simply to *believe* it. And that's the purpose of coming to the Book. It is to lead to determined faithfulness, to a change of lifestyle. The test of the value of something like the Keswick Convention is not so much whether we are stirred emotionally, but whether or not, as a result of our exposure to God's Word, we become more obedient.

If we're concerned about the welfare of our families and our children, if we are concerned about the moral and spiritual well-being of our nations, and if we are determined to play our part in God's purposes of restoration, then we must be people ready to respond to God's Word, committed to live the truth. As D. L. Moody used to say, 'Every Bible needs to be bound with shoe leather.'

5. Living by God's Standards
Nehemiah 10 & 13

Mention the word *perestroika* in Russia today, and you are usually greeted with cynicism. The reason is obvious. In his book, *Perestroika*, the then President Gorbachev made frequent reference to the credibility gap between words and deeds. He insisted that people did not want political slogans that failed to square with reality. *Perestroika* meant 'the unity of words and deeds', and on that basis Gorbachev attempted to reform the Soviet system. It was a noble aim – but for the Russian people its failure was painfully evident. The unity between political promises and economic and social reality was a myth. And therein lay Gorbachev's downfall, with Yeltsin's following soon after.

We're suspicious of manifesto pledges and political programmes at the best of times and when there is no genuine change we become cynical about the entire process. Charles Handy, the business guru, says, 'The leader must live the vision.' He must put his money where his mouth is. This is effectively what John wrote: 'Whoever claims to live in him must walk as Jesus did' (1 Jn. 2:6). It is a matter of faith that works, truth in action, godliness in working clothes.

Christians in the first century couldn't afford inconsistency. As we read the New Testament we see the close connection between holiness and mission. The early church was being watched; their lives, their work, their families, their values, their response under pressure – all of these had to support their radical message. This was nothing new for those who were called to be God's people. It was a major Old Testament theme. And as we come to the closing chapters of the book of Nehemiah we see that, at the heart of the process of the rebuilding of God's people, there lay a concern for absolute consistency. God's people were to live by God's standards.

In this regard their uniqueness as a community – their distinct morality, social and economic relationships and life-style – was to be a witness to the character of the God whom they worshipped. We have already touched on this theme in Nehemiah 5, but now, in chapter 10, we come to the special agreement made by the people, the renewal of the covenant relationship, in which they affirm their 'distinctness'.

> The rest of the people – priests, Levites, gatekeepers, singers, temple servants and all who separated themselves from the neighbouring peoples for the sake of the Law of God, to-gether with their wives and all their sons and daughters who are able to understand – all these now join their brothers and the nobles, and bind themselves with a curse and an oath to follow the Law of God given through Moses the servant of God and to obey carefully all the commands, regulations and decrees of the Lord our Lord (10:28–29).

It is a misunderstanding to think that being 'separated from the peoples' might suggest an elitist or exclusivist mentality. The separation being spoken about was a religious separation. The peoples of neighbouring lands worshipped other gods, and so the call to be separate and distinct came from the first commandment: 'You shall have no other gods before me.' It was a declaration of their allegiance to Yahweh. But more than that, the text indicates it was all those who had separated themselves 'to the Law of God' (10:28). The way in which they lived would demonstrate their commitment to that one Lord and would be a witness to their neighbours of what the true God was like.

Belief matched by behaviour is as fundamental today for effective mission as it was then. We face the challenge of chapter 10, where the people declare their commitment to

God's standards, and of chapter 13, where we find promise without performance.

1) Commitment to God's standards (chapter 10)

In response to the reading of God's Word, the people make a solemn undertaking to live according to God's laws, with a number of specific resolutions to be faithful (10:30 onwards). I have selected three:

a) The identity of God's people

'We promise not to give our daughters in marriage to the peoples around us or take their daughters for our sons' (10:30). When the urge to merge is a universal phenomenon, why do the people support a restriction? As we've seen, the kind of separation being called for was for religious not for racial reasons. The Old Testament law made it clear: you can't possibly have a strong marriage if husband and wife are worshipping different gods. Compromise would be inevitable for the follower of Yahweh, who makes exclusive claims on His people. Malachi used strong idiomatic language to condemn this kind of behaviour: 'Judah has desecrated the sanctuary the Lord loves by marrying the daughter of a foreign god' (Mal. 2:11). He was deeply concerned to sustain the identity of God's people, around whom God's purposes of redemption were focused. This kind of inter-marriage would lead to a loss of faithfulness to the one Lord, and a gradual erosion of the uniqueness of God's people. Compromise would have disastrous consequences. So the people affirmed that they would live by God's standards.

b) The significance of God's covenant

'When the neighbouring peoples bring merchandise or grain to sell on the Sabbath, we will not buy from them on the Sabbath or on any holy day. Every seventh year we will forgo working the land and will cancel all debts' (10:31).

The Old Testament law had established several vital reasons why observing the Sabbath was at the heart of their distinctness as a nation. As a day of rest, it went right back to the pattern of God's work and rest in creation, when it was also set aside to reflect on God's goodness and to worship Him. It was a day when the people acknowledged that God could continue to provide for their needs, even when they were not working, and was therefore a declaration of their allegiance to the Lord, and their trust in His covenant promises to be faithful in His care for them. The temptation now, in Jerusalem, was to soft-pedal that idea.

Again, it's important to remember the circumstances. The exiles had come back to a gloomy situation. There was a huge amount to be done in the fields, many had not yet returned, much of the land was occupied by others, the economy was struggling. There were foreign traders ready and willing to develop their market, even on the Sabbath. But on that day of national re-dedication, moved by God's Word and God's Spirit, the people were determined to express their loyalty to the teaching on the Sabbath. They would trust Him fully to care for them.

c) The priority of God's house

The rest of chapter 10:32–39 is a statement of the people's commitment to the upkeep of the temple. Again, this goes back to many references to the Law (Exodus 30), and the people now recognized their individual responsibility to give annually to sustain the ministry of the temple, which was right at the heart of the city, and represented their relationship with God Himself. That's why they had worked so hard to rebuild the city and restore the temple. This was the place where God was to be worshipped. This was to be their number one priority. They were to give: money (v. 32), grain (v. 33), wood for the altar (v. 34), first fruits of their crops (v. 35) and tithes (vv. 37–39) to support the priests and the Levites. 'We will not neglect the house of our God,' they said, knowing that if the temple went down, so would their relationship with God. Their commitment was substantial. It involved every family, it impacted their day-to-day life and it was a continuing obligation to acknowledge that everything they had belonged to God. Giving the first fruits of their crops declared that this was their first priority, the first call on their resources.

Their agreement in chapter 10 struck at the heart of what it meant to be God's people: a distinct, holy nation, committed to the one God, trusting His faithfulness for every aspect of life. They were going to obey Him at all costs, and trust Him to keep 'his covenant of love'. However, that is not what happened. I'm sure you've heard the illustration of the frog and the kettle. If you place a frog in hot water it will immediately jump out and save its skin. But if you place a frog in cold water and gradually heat the water, the frog won't notice what's happening and will boil to death.

Trying to live lives of committed Christian discipleship in today's world demands constant vigilance, constant dependence on the power of God's Word and Spirit. We face the daily pressure to conform to the world's standards, the subtle and insidious influence of secularism. We hardly notice the drift away from God's standards, the dilution of our committed resolve to be followers of Jesus Christ. As God's people, we gradually lose our distinctness and it was no different in Nehemiah's day: that is exactly the situation he encountered towards the end of his leadership in Jerusalem. After his first term as governor, Nehemiah had returned to Susa to fulfil his responsibilities for King Artaxerxes. When he came back to Jerusalem for a second term as governor, about 20 years after the people had made their solemn commitments in chapter 10, he would have been around 65 years old, but instead of coming home to retire, Nehemiah discovered that his work was not over. His motto was, 'I've started, so I'll finish.' By chapter 13, we discover that a terrible spiritual decline had set in. Far from sustaining their distinctness as God's people, they had drifted away from God's standards. After all of the promises, there was no performance.

2) Promise without performance (chapter 13)

After the incredible feat of rebuilding of the wall, after revival in the city at the reading of God's Word, after the solemn and binding commitments made by the people in the service of covenant renewal, Nehemiah returns to discover a self-serving bunch of individualists, not the dedicated people of God. We are given a very realistic view of what can happen and a very human insight into the struggles Nehemiah faced in urging the people to remain faithful. Many contemporary expressions of Christian hope for revival imagine that it will be instantaneous – that God will change me, the church, and society as if by a magic wand.

Chuck Swindoll tells the story of a family from the backwoods who went to the city for the first time in their lives to stay in a hotel. On arrival, the man told his wife to stay in the truck while he and Junior checked the hotel. They were fascinated by a small room with doors that slid open at the centre. People would walk up, press the button and wait. The lights would flicker, then the doors would slide open. People would walk in, turn round, and click – the doors closed. Then a little old lady shuffled up to the doors. She pushed the button and waited for a few seconds. The doors opened, the old lady hobbled into the little room. There was no one else with her, and the doors closed. Then just 30 seconds later, the doors opened again – and there stood a stunning young blonde. She had the perfect body, a wonderful smile. As she stepped out and walked past them, the father nudged his boy and said, 'Hey Junior, go get Mama!'

There are no buttons to press for automatic renewal in the Christian life! There might be a tendency, in contemporary evangelicalism, to be attracted to apparently quick-fix solutions to our corporate problems, miraculous interventions or slick strategies that will deliver growth and renewal. But there are no such instant solutions. There is instead what one writer has called 'a long obedience in the same direction' – a firm and disciplined commitment to trust God's Word, depend on God's Spirit and live in God's community. Otherwise there will be drift towards compromise and decay. What did Nehemiah discover on his return to Jerusalem? We will look at exactly the same three themes that we earlier examined.

a) The priority of God's house – and the result of indifference

Verses 4–9 re-introduce us to Nehemiah's old enemy Tobiah, whom we saw in chapters 4 and 6. With good social and political connections in the city, he had, by now, infiltrated to such an extent that even the high priest Eliashib had offered him favours, 'He had provided Tobiah with a large room formerly used to store the grain offerings and incense and temple articles, and also the tithes of grain, new wine and oil prescribed for the Levites, the singers and gatekeepers, as well as the contributions for the priests' (v. 5). When Nehemiah discovered this he was furious. Apart from the strategic danger from this kind of insidious infiltration, Tobiah was a layman and had no right to be in the temple. Taking over the storeroom had resulted in ceremonial defilement.

And behind this incident was another serious issue. Eliashib had apparently been happy to give Tobiah the temple room because it wasn't needed for its purpose of storage – tithing had gradually declined, and as Nehemiah recorded, 'I also learned that the portions assigned to the Levites had not been given to them, and that all the Levites and singers responsible for the service had gone back to their own fields' (v. 10). The Levites depended on the gifts for their income and now that had dried up they had to go out and work the fields, and so the temple services were being neglected.

Acting decisively, Nehemiah says, 'I was greatly displeased and threw all Tobiah's household goods out of the room. I gave orders to purify the rooms, and then I put back into them the equipment of the house of God, with the grain offerings and the incense' (v. 8). It's a reminder of Jesus' own determination to honour God's house when he made a whip and drove out the money changers from the temple area. 'How dare you turn my Father's house into a market?' (Jn. 2:16). That's also Nehemiah's passion: 'So I rebuked the officials and asked them, "Why is the house of God neglected?"' (v. 11). Do you remember the last verse of chapter 10? 'We will not neglect the house of our God.' Promise without performance. They had become indifferent to the priority of that commitment to God's work, so Nehemiah appoints trustworthy men to be in charge of the storerooms (v. 13), to ensure that the pledges made 20 years earlier were going to be fulfilled.

Of course, our situation is very different from the fifth century BC. But the New Testament teaches us that both the Christian and the church are God's temple, indwelt by the Spirit. And it is all too easy for there to be defilement right at the heart of that temple. 'Besetting sins, unhallowed relationships, the self-serving pursuit of pleasure, profit, power, or position, unconcern about pleasing and glorifying God, and any pattern of action that in any way undermines obedience to God's written Word and fidelity to the Christ of the Scriptures has a defiling effect in God's sight,' says J. I. Packer. And if that is something we have come to realize in our lives or in our churches, then Nehemiah's actions are also examples for us: remove the bad, restore the good.

One of the main lessons of this chapter is that we need to be watching out for those things that can produce an indifference to God's cause. We can so easily be affected by the materialism of our day, where personal wealth displaces the things of God. We neglect the priority of God's work in some way, and that is soon exploited by a Tobiah, who secures his toehold and begins the process of defilement.

b) The significance of God's covenant – and the drift towards expediency

Verses 15–22 describe the next disappointment for Nehemiah. We have seen from chapter 10 why the command to honour the Sabbath regulations was a significant call to God's people to remain distinct, to be God's covenant community. Nehemiah had urged a rigorous enforcement of that law. And what did he find 20 years later? 'In those days I saw men in Judah treading winepresses on the Sabbath and bringing in grain and loading it on donkeys, together with wine, grapes, figs and all other kinds of loads. They were bringing all this into Jerusalem on the Sabbath' (v. 15). And in verse 16 Phoenician merchants were setting up their stalls at the Fish Gate and trading on the Sabbath. As the people became indifferent to God's house, they had also turned their backs on their earlier commitment to the Sabbath by a drift towards commercial expediency. When Gentile traders arrived in Jerusalem, they found nothing distinct about the nation, no devotion or loyalty on the part of the so-called people of God.

Again Nehemiah rebukes the leaders in Jerusalem: 'What is this wicked thing you are doing – desecrating the Sabbath day?' (v. 17). And he warns them of the potentially disastrous consequences. It was precisely because of their forefathers' failure to honour the covenant that Jerusalem had been destroyed by the Babylonians and the people had been carted off into exile. So history was in danger of repeating itself. Nehemiah's determined action (vv. 19–21) shows a man who is totally committed to sustaining God's standards, who refuses to accept a drift towards an easy religion, where faith is shaped by personal expediency rather than godly determination. Nehemiah saw that the decision to ignore the Sabbath was a denial of faith in God.

Again, what are we to make of this in the twenty-first century? Much has been written about the way Christians view the Sabbath, or how they should treat Sunday. What is clear from Scripture, as a whole, is that this special day is an important paradigm for Christians. Both creation and redemption remind us of its importance. As a creation ordinance we see it as part of the rhythm of our lives when God has made us rest from our usual labours. But if we fail to take the creation ordinance seriously, we will find it will impact our whole lives. And this is coupled with the importance of the Lord's Day as the day of spiritual refreshment and renewal, the day for honouring and worshipping God with a distinctness that marks us out as His people.

We are not under Old Testament Sabbath laws and we should not be put off by what we sometimes call the neo-Sabbatarians who try to import much of the old covenant into the new. However, that does not mean that the Lord's Day has no significance for Christians. It is not easy to balance all the demands of life in our sophisticated society, but we need to find ways of ensuring that we affirm that the Son of Man is Lord of the Sabbath. That includes the essential priority of worship with God's people and the importance of spiritual renewal. The Puritan Thomas Watson wrote, 'When the falling dust of the world has clogged the wheels of our affections so that they can scarcely move towards God, the Sabbath/Sunday comes and oils the wheels of our own affections and they move swiftly on.'

Actually, Sundays can be pretty crazy days for many of us. We live as though Jesus had said in John, 'I am come that you might have meetings, meetings in their abundance!' What matters is that our commitment to worship, rest and celebration, in whatever way is legitimate for us, is consistent with God's standards. Our ordering of our priorities, our time with the family, or our commitment to care for others – all of these are signals to those around us that we are part of God's new society. This will become more and more difficult as our societies drift towards secularism, but it will be an essential ingredient for the health of our souls and bodies, the health of our churches and perhaps too, the health of the societies we are able to influence for good.

c) The identity of God's people – and the danger of compromise

How must Nehemiah have been feeling as he encountered a third area where promise had not been matched by performance? 'Moreover, in those days I saw men of Judah who had married women from Ashdod, Ammon and Moab. Half of their children spoke the language of Ashdod or the language of one of the other peoples, and did not know how to speak the language of Judah' (v. 23).

Marrying people of other nations, as we have seen, was a threat to the solidarity and identity of God's own people. It was this that Nehemiah saw most clearly when he returned to Jerusalem. The danger to the next generation was that the Israelite identity would be eroded because the children could not understand God's Word and their uniqueness as followers of the one Lord would gradually be dissolved. It seemed to Nehemiah that everyone in Jerusalem was involved in such inter-marriage, including the hopelessly compromised leadership in the city. So again he took what might seem to be drastic action (v. 25), rebuking the leaders and making them promise not to pursue such disastrous compromise. Don't put your family at risk and don't put God's people at risk.

As we've seen, there were special reasons why the Old Testament stresses this theme, to do with the identity of the nation and God's purposes of redemption. So application of these verses needs to be handled with care and with sensitivity. They are not to be used as arguments against cross-cultural marriage amongst Christians, nor are they to be used to make a Christian who has a non-Christian partner feel compromised, for reasons Paul explains in 1 Corinthians 7:12–16. Some Christians find themselves unavoidably in this situation and they are encouraged here and also in 1 Peter 3 to see that this represents an important opportunity for them: '… if any of them do not believe the word, they may be won over without words by the behaviour of their wives, when they see the purity and reverence of your lives' (1 Pet. 3:1, 2).

But nevertheless, Paul is very clear that, in making the decision to marry, the partner we Christians choose must 'belong to the Lord' (1 Cor. 7:39). He or she must be a believer. In other words, for us Christians there is still a covenant relationship with God. Note Paul's words in 2 Corinthians 6. He begins with a call in verse 14 not to be 'yoked together with unbelievers', a picture borrowed from the book of Deuteronomy, where the law forbade ploughing a field using different kinds of animals working together – an ox and a donkey would pull at different speeds and so they would be ineffective harnessed together. This was one example of several instances in the Old Testament law where God's people were required to act consistently. Just as there should be no mismatch when ploughing a field, so there should be no mixing of crops in the field, no mixing of different fibres in their home-spun cloth, and for the people themselves, no contamination with their pagan neighbours.

And it seems a legitimate application of Paul's call for consistent Christian living, to say that he is calling us to avoid the wrong kind of marriage partnership. If becoming a Christian means your whole view of life changes – different values, different ambitions, different ethical standards and, most importantly, a different authority in your life – how can you share your life intimately with someone outside of God's family? How can you be 'at one'? 'What does a believer have in common with an unbeliever?' (v. 15). Painful as it might be initially, the Christian is called to avoid any close liaison, including marriage, which will compromise the distinctness of their calling. Keep alert to the danger of compromise. Make Jesus the number one priority.

Conclusions

a) Christian integrity

This chapter could not be more relevant to the twenty-first-century church. We face the constant temptation to compromise with the world. Its seductive appeal comes in many forms, pressurizing us to conform in relationships, business, sexuality, materialism, ambition and lifestyle. But as God's new society, our task is to *challenge* the world, not *conform* to it. And to do that we need the empowering of God's Spirit and the truth of God's Word. Francis Schaeffer used to call Christians to live consistently with the Word God has given, in the world God has made. And as in the fifth century BC, the distinctness of God's people will result in effective witness to the God to whom we belong. We live our lives before a watching world. As Peter reminds us, 'Live such good lives amongst the pagans that, though they accuse you of doing wrong, they may see your good deeds and glorify God on the day he visits us' (1 Pet. 2:12).

b) Christian perseverance

Comparing chapters 10 and 13 of Nehemiah reminds us of one of the most important gifts of the Spirit – the gift of perseverance: the ability, having put our hand to the plough, to keep cutting a straight furrow. As commentators rightly say about these chapters, they remind us that the church can take nothing for granted. As the Reformers of the sixteenth century stressed, the church needs always to be reformed, and this will continue to be the case until we reach heaven. So we must call one another, in the church of God, to be constantly vigilant, constantly living under the authority of Scripture, constantly seeking the Spirit's help in our commitment to obey.

Nehemiah was determined, as we see from his short prayers in chapter 13, that he would be remembered for faithfulness not failure. That's what we want, isn't it? 'I have fought the good fight, I have finished the race, I have kept the faith. Now there is in store for me a crown of righteousness, which the Lord, the righteous Judge, will award to me on that day – and not only to me, but also to all who have longed for his appearing' (2 Tim 4:7–8).

That brings us to the final conclusion. We have:

c) Christian hope

The story of Nehemiah is a story of human fickleness and of God's faithfulness. We began in Nehemiah's prayer in chapter 1 with the reminder of God's purposes: 'If you return to me and obey my commands, then even if your exiled people are at the farthest horizon, I will gather them from there and bring them to the place I have chosen as a dwelling for my Name' (1:9). And in part, that happened. But we have seen only a shadow of the ultimate reality of which that prayer speaks. By the close of Nehemiah 13 we have not yet seen the promised spiritual restoration. In AD 70 the Romans destroyed the walls and the temple once again. And the story of the unfaithfulness of God's people is a recurring theme.

Something totally new would be required, as Jeremiah predicted in his promise of a new covenant. In Jesus himself, God would fulfil His promises to restore His people, not now defined by walls or a temple, not now restricted in its membership, but made up of men and women from every nation and tribe and tongue and people. It is in Him that all of God's promises are finally fulfilled. Right now, as C.S. Lewis observed, we Christians live in the 'Shadowlands'. But it will not always be like that and until we reach heaven, we need to live our lives with utter devotion to the Lord as a distinctive community honouring His name. We do so with our hearts and minds fixed on our eternal home, our destiny as the people of God.

John's vision in Revelation 21 of a New Jerusalem is surely the place to conclude. He sees a city, with its gates never shut (v. 25), with nothing impure entering (v. 27), with no enemies threatening it:

> … the Holy City, the new Jerusalem coming down out of heaven from God, prepared as a bride beautifully dressed for her husband. And I heard a loud voice from the throne saying, 'Now the dwelling of God is with men, and he will live with them. They will be his people, and God himself will be with them and be their God. He will wipe every tear from their eyes. There will be no more death or mourning or crying or pain, for the old order of things has passed away (Rev. 21:2–4).

Even so, come Lord Jesus.

The Addresses

Fire Quenchers
by Ann Graham Lotz

Revelation 2–3

In 1859 revival broke out in Northern Ireland, swept through Wales, Scotland and England, and as a result thousands of people were convicted of sin, repented of sin, placed their faith in Jesus Christ as Saviour and had their lives transformed. Now, in the year 2000, three generations later, where is the impact? I've travelled in the United Kingdom and seen something here that is the same in America: we seem, as a remnant of believers, to be shrinking. We look back to revivals, but where is the revival today? We know that Jesus promised us, in Acts 1:8, that we would receive power when the Holy Spirit comes upon us. And Paul told Timothy in 2 Timothy 1: you have received the Holy Spirit, you have received the fire of God and His power when I laid my hands on you at your conversion, but Timothy, it's your responsibility to fan Him into flame. I wonder if the Holy Spirit, the fire of God and the power of God has been allowed to die out in our midst. Why does it seem to be that we cannot pass the revival fires from one generation to the next? And often we cannot even pass that fire on within our own home to our own children.

In Roman days people didn't have a switch to turn on lights in their home, or gas to light their stove, or something to start their fire with, they had a central plaza in every village where a fire was kept burning. If you wanted to light the lamps or the stove in your home you went to the fire in the central plaza, took a brand of fire from it and took it home. The village considered the fire so important that they hired a full-time firekeeper, just to keep the fire burning. If the firekeeper allowed the fire to go out for any reason, if a rainstorm came along and drenched it, or the wind came along and blew it out, or the firekeeper just went to sleep and let the fire burn out, it cost the firekeeper his life. It was considered vitally important to the life of the community that the fire always be kept burning. And I believe Paul was saying, 'Timothy, you are the firekeeper and you've got to make sure that the fire of the Holy Spirit is maintained in your heart and maintained in your life.'

I want to examine some of the *fire quenchers* in our lives and hearts which put the fire out. Of course, when you receive Christ by faith as your Saviour He comes into your life in the person of the Holy Spirit. And the Holy Spirit, once He comes into your heart and life, will never leave you; He will never forsake you. You are sealed forever. But our sin and our disobedience can quench and grieve the Holy Spirit, who is so quiet and still within us, we can think we have lost our salvation and the fire will go out. Or at least, it will be just a flicker instead of the burning flame that it is supposed to be. In Revelation 2 and 3 Jesus writes to seven different churches and in each one of these letters I see a fire quencher. And I am going to share with you personally some of the fire quenchers that I have had to deal with.

1) The church at Ephesus (Rev. 2:1–7)

Let me describe Ephesus to you. The church there had been pastored by the apostle Paul and the apostle John and it was under the supervision of Timothy. Most of the people in the church, when this letter was written, had been born and raised in a Christian home. They were in their second generation of knowing Christ. Right there I identify with the Ephesian church because I have been exposed to outstanding Bible teachers and preachers and I was raised in a Christian home. Does that apply to you? I know if you have been coming to Keswick for any length of time you have also been exposed to outstanding Bible teachers and preachers. And I expect, just from my conversations with many of you, that most of you have been raised in a Christian home, you have a lot of knowledge and are very familiar with the Christian traditions.

What our Lord saw in the Ephesian church He may see in you also. I know He sees it in me. And so He begins, 'To the angel of the church in Ephesus write: These are the words of him who holds the seven stars in his right hand and walks among the seven golden lampstands.' He begins each one of these letters the same way, by focusing the attention of the believers onto Himself. He is saying, *Look at Me*, I hold the stars in My right hand – and we know from the end of chapter 1 that the stars are the leaders of the church, they represent you and me. You can think of Him holding you in His hand as He walks amongst the lampstands; He's in our midst. I believe He holds you and me in His right hand because He wants to use us. I hold the instruments I use in my right hand – my pencil, my comb, my fork – and He is wanting to use you and me to glorify Him, to pass the gospel and the reality of Christ on to the next generation. He is saying, I am here tonight, I am walking in your midst, I am present with you, will you look at me?

And sometimes it is easy, in a Convention like this, to look at everyone around us or the person on the platform and the Lord would tell us, not just tonight but every time we gather, 'Keep your focus on Jesus. *Look at me.*'

Secondly, He says, *Learn from me*. He says, I know what you are doing right, and the Ephesian church was doing many things right, I know your deeds, your hard work, your perseverance. I know that you cannot tolerate wicked men, that you have tested those who claim to be apostles but are not, and have found them false. You have persevered and have endured hardships for my name, you have not grown weary (v. 2), and now in verse 6, you hate what I hate. I think that describes the congregation of the Keswick Convention. And I believe the Lord would tell you that He knows your deeds. He knows your hard work. He knows that you are the remnant in the United Kingdom and He knows how busy you are. But you have made the time to draw aside, to listen to his word and bring your family to this Convention, and I believe that the Lord has brought me from America, if nothing else, to say this evening, 'Thank you.'

There are many things that you and I do for the Lord Jesus Christ that nobody else knows about, especially as a wife and mother. We do a lot of things in the kitchen, in the house, for our children and nobody notices, nobody thanks us, and the Lord says, 'I know your deeds. I know you even do your housework as unto Me.' And then there are things in the church behind the scenes, in the kitchen, in the parking lot. Just turning on the lights, turning on the heat, administrative responsibilities nobody knows about, but the Lord says, 'I know.' And He says, 'Thank you.' And I think this letter opens with heaven's applause. If the Lord applauds you tonight, would you receive His applause and commendation? He knows your deeds and your hard work and the sacrifices and struggles to get you here and He says, 'Thank you for all that you are doing for Me.'

Then secondly, He says, 'I not only know what you are doing right, but I know something that you are doing wrong.' 'Yet I hold this against you: You have forsaken your first love' (v. 4). All three of my children got married within eight months of each other and as you can imagine, there is a lot of first love around our house! First love is emotional, passionate and affectionate. I can remember when I fell in love with my husband, I just wanted to be with him all the time and to talk to him all the time. I hung on every word he said and couldn't have enough of him. When he wasn't with me I would talk to other people about him. I was almost obnoxious, talking to everybody about Danny Lotz. I was in love and when you fall in love with Jesus it's the same, isn't it? You just can't talk to Him enough, you spend hours in prayer and it isn't long enough. You want to hear every word He has to say. You can't read enough of your Bible and then you are almost obnoxious, telling everybody about Jesus, witnessing and sharing Christ.

When did you lose it? When did you lose being in love with Jesus?

One of the impressions I have about the Ephesian church is that they were busy – all of their good deeds, all of their hard work, all of their persevering. And I wonder, did they fall in love with Jesus? When you fall in love you just want to do something for the person to show them how much you love them. Maybe these Ephesian Christians, as they fell in love with Jesus, thought they wanted to do something for Jesus and they began to serve Him and then wanted to serve Him more. Pretty soon people found out these people will work in the church and so they gave them more to do, until they are so *busy* serving, so *busy* working for Him, they don't have time for Him and somewhere along the line they lost their love.

I taught a Bible class in my home town for 12 years. I was just so hungry to know God's word and you really learn it when you have to teach it. Then God called me to accept invitations around the world and share His word in an itinerant ministry. One of the first invitations I received was to lead a pastors' conference in Fiji. Then I was invited to go to a pastors' conference in Brazil. Someone heard I was in Brazil and invited me to a youth conference in southern Brazil. I went there and came back to America. I was travelling around speaking and I knew when I prayed I no longer seemed to get through; I knew when I went to church, I no longer seemed to enter into worship; I knew when I read my Bible I no longer seemed to hear His voice, but I thought I was just tired and jet lagged.

Then one day I was reading these verses and God said to me, 'Ann, I know your deeds, I know your hard work, your perseverance,' and He went right on down the list. 'You have been to Fiji and you have been ... Thank you for just wanting to share my word and bring other people into it. Ann, I have something against you. You are losing your love for me.' I just went on to the next verse. I knew that wasn't me because I went all round the world telling other people how they could love Jesus. But when Jesus begins to convict you about something you can't get away from that verse; He keeps bringing you back and back to it. Finally I listened. I knew that He had seen something in my heart that I hadn't seen in myself. He was saying, 'Ann, you are losing your love for me. In all of your busyness you are not making time for me.' And I can remember getting on my knees and the tears coming down my cheeks. 'Lord, I am so sorry. What do I do?'

And he told me three things.

a) 'Remember the height from which you have fallen' (v. 5). I think the pinnacle of the Christian life is being in love with Jesus. I could remember the height. Do you remember being in love with Jesus? Do you remember what it was like to spend hours in prayer and in His word and share the gospel and be so excited to serve? I could remember and He said, 'Ann, remember the height from which you have fallen, fallen in your usefulness to me, fallen in your testimony, fallen in your relationship with me.' And then He said:

b) 'Repent' (v. 5), and repentance means to stop it. If a first love is emotional, affectionate, passionate, we can't control those things. How do you stop not having them? How can I get them back? And so I asked the Lord, 'Lord, I am willing to repent, but how do I get back that first love?' And so He said:

c) 'Return to the first things.' And I said, 'Lord, what first things?' And He took me back in my mind, by faith, to the cross where I first knew Jesus as my Saviour and I was first aware of His death on the cross and what it cost Him to take away my sin and bring me into that personal love relationship with Himself. And I fell on my face in prayer before Him, at the cross, and thanked Him all over again for what the Lord of Glory did, leaving the throne in heaven, humbling Himself and becoming a servant, being obedient even to death on the cross, that He might take away my sin. If no one else had benefited, He would still have gone to the cross just for me. He shed His own blood for my sin and I went back to the cross. Would you do that? Just go back by faith to the cross.

And then the Lord said, 'Ann, return not only to the cross, but to what you were doing at first, when you were in love with me, that you are not doing now.' And I knew immediately what it was. Can you remember what it was like to love Jesus with all of your heart, mind, soul and strength, and what were you doing then, that you are not doing now? Were you spending time in prayer with Him? Were you spending time reading and meditating on the Scriptures? Were you spending time sharing the gospel? Were you spending time in a certain fellowship? What were you doing, that you are not doing now? He says, return to those first things. For me, I realized I had been going around the world giving out messages that I had already prepared and I had not been doing any in-depth Bible studies for myself. That very day I began doing a study of the book of Revelation and this message is part of the fruit of my repentance. My book, *The Vision of His Glory*, is the result of my repentance before God. Within a week the joy was back, the sense of His presence, an awareness of His love for me. Oh, I pray I will never again lose my first love.

I wonder if there was something in your life that you let slip out like I did. Or maybe there was something that wasn't in your life, when you were in love with Jesus, that you have allowed to slide in: a habit, an attitude, a wrong relationship, in other words, just sin. And sin will kill your love for Jesus quicker than anything. You need to take it to the cross and crucify it. Whatever it is, it is not worth your love relationship with Jesus. Jesus said, 'Ann, I want you to remember the height from which you have fallen and repent of not loving me. And I want you to return to the first things.'

Then He gave me a little motivation in case I hesitated, 'If you do not repent I will come to you and remove your lampstand from its place' (v. 5). The lampstand is the church. I don't think it means He is going to physically remove the church from the neighbourhood, but that He will remove Himself from the church. I have been in many churches in America with beautiful facilities, but the Spirit of Jesus is not there. He has left because they have not maintained that fire of love for Him in their hearts.

But I also took this verse personally because a lampstand is a stand on which you place a lamp, allowing the light to go in broader spectrum, and I felt that lampstand was my ministry. It allows me to have a broader area of influence and I felt He was saying, 'Ann, if you don't put love for Me back first in your heart and in your life, I am going to dry up your ministry.' I don't have an agent or a brochure to get me appointments, I just trust God to open the doors and He could dry it up just like that. There was a time in my life when I was scared to death He would call me into service. Then there came a point when I was scared to death He would not call me into service! I love the Lord and I want to serve Him and in order to serve Him, according to His will and His way, He has to open the doors for me. And He was saying, 'Ann, I will shut them tight if you don't repent.' And so I repented.

I wonder, is there someone here tonight, busy, busy, busy? So active in church, involved in so many things. And the Lord would say, 'Thank you.' So many people are complacent and apathetic and the Lord says, 'Thank you for all your busyness in My Name, but I hold something against you: you are so busy serving Me, you are not making time for Me. You've lost your love for Me. Would you repent of your lovelessness?' Then He says, '*Listen to Me.* Listen to what the Spirit is saying.' There is a principle here: the Lord Jesus Christ wants our love for Him more than all of our service and obedience combined. What is the first and greatest commandment? That we 'love the Lord our God with all our heart, soul, mind and strength'. He knows when we love Him like that, the rest will fall into place. Love must come first. Are you putting your work before your worship? Put your worship first and, as you worship, your work flows from your worship.

The promise is this, 'He who has an ear, let him hear what the Spirit says to the churches. To him who overcomes I will give the right to eat of the tree of life which is in the paradise of God' (v. 7). The tree of life represents eternal life which includes our love for Him and His love for us and an awareness of His love. The paradise of God is His presence and the promise is this: you can eat of that tree and be deeply satisfied in a precious, permanent love relationship with Jesus Christ and live in awareness of His presence, if you'll just put worship first. Do you have an ear to hear what the Spirit is saying?

There is *a fire quencher of busyness* and *a fire quencher of passionless service* when you place your work before your worship. Will you put love for Jesus back first in your life? The church at Ephesus did not listen. I've walked through the ruins. There is no Christian church in Ephesus today. The revival fire died out.

2) The church at Smyrna (Rev. 2:8–11)

I see the *fire quencher of fearfulness* in her life because she was so afraid of persecution and criticism in a pluralistic society. She was afraid of sharing the gospel. And so our Lord said, 'Don't be afraid.'

3) The church at Pergamum (Rev. 2:12–17)

Here we see *the fire quencher of shallowness* – allowing other people to come in the church and deceive you and draw you away from a simple faith in God's Word. I am assuming that in this church they had people who were preaching 'health and wealth and prosperity' or some ecstatic emotional experience, or they were preaching that this Book contains the Word of God but isn't the Word of God from cover to cover, and they just led people away from faith in God's Word. There was a shallowness. John Stott said that the church of God is growing phenomenally all over the world, but it's growing so shallow, there's no depth. Shallowness is a fire quencher; you can't pass the reality of your faith in Jesus Christ to the next generation if you are shallow in your faith. It needs to be rooted in God's Word.

4) The church of Thyatira (Rev. 2:18–29)

I'd probably expound on this to an American audience – *the fire quencher of permissiveness*. They allowed immorality within the church, until pretty soon you couldn't tell a worldling from a church member, their lifestyles were so similar. Immorality either in your life or in your thought process, the things you watch on TV, the magazines that you read, will put the fire out.

5) The church at Sardis (Rev. 3:1–6)

There are two fire quenchers in this church: *prayerlessness* and *phoniness* 'To the angel of the church in Sardis write: These are the words of him who holds the seven spirits of God and seven stars.' Jesus begins by saying, 'Look at me,' and the picture He gives of Himself is someone who is holding the balance scales. On one side is the sevenfold Spirit of God, the Holy Spirit, and on the other side is the church. Some people believe they are going to heaven and when they get there God will let them in because He will weigh their good works against their bad works, and if there are more good things than bad things then God will let them into heaven. They have got something right – God is going to weigh them – but He doesn't weigh our good works against our bad works, He weighs our entire lives against the perfection of the Holy Spirit. He weighs the church at Sardis and He says, 'You don't measure up.' He says, '*Look at Me.* I am the One to whom you are accountable, I am the One who will judge your life, I am the One who holds the scales. Are you looking?'

'*Learn from Me,*' He says, 'I know what you are doing right.' He really searched hard to find something He could commend them for. For he says, 'You have a few people in Sardis who have not soiled their clothes and they walk with me' (v. 4). He was commending the church of Sardis for knowing some people who were right with Him, and that's the only thing He could commend them for. They were doing wrong: 'I know your deeds; you have a reputation of being alive but you are dead' (v. 1). The church at Sardis was filled with Bible quoters, Bible toters, living out their Christian lives to impress other people, caring more about the opinions of other church members than caring about the opinion of God. They were phoneys, they weren't real.

I can remember the time and the place when God convicted me of this. It was when I was seventeen years old; maybe there is a young person who needs to hear this. I was so bound by the fact that I was Billy Graham's daughter and everybody had an idea of what Billy Graham's daughter ought to be like and dress like, act like, who her friends ought to be and the places she ought to go. They were always trying to press me into their moulds and because I didn't want to embarrass my daddy, I wanted to be an asset, I tried to please everybody. When I was with this group I was one thing and when I was with another group I was that way. Just like a spiritual chameleon – changing colours with everyone I was with. Finally, in the summer of my seventeenth year, somebody grabbed me and said, 'Ann, you are looking at God through a prism and your relationship with God is coloured by everyone else's opinion. You need to look at God directly.' And right there on that dusty road in Southern California I thought, 'All right, God, I am just going to live my life for You and I am not going to care what other people think. I am just going to live my life to please You. I know that if I live my life to please You, my parents are going to be pleased and my grandparents are going to be pleased and the people I care most about are going to be pleased. And some people won't be pleased, but I can't please everybody anyway, so I am just going to live my life to please You.' I can't tell you what a freeing thing that was.

Tonight, as nervous as I am, in a sense I really don't care what you think because I speak for an audience of One. If I am faithful to the message that God has put on my heart, and if I render it to the best of my ability (and I know I make a lot of mistakes), then God will be pleased. And if you are not, I'm sorry. Do you understand? If you bump into me in the market square or at the hotel, you are going to see me like I am, I don't change. I am just myself and I live my life every moment to please God. Is there somebody here living your Christian life to impress other people? That's a fire quencher, especially within the home, isn't it? Your children are the first to see you putting on a show for the outside world. You say nasty things about people and when they come to your door you open it and say, 'Welcome, so glad to see you.' And your children get the message, don't they!

My grandparents helped raise me, because I was pretty much raised by a single parent and I stayed many nights with them. No matter what time I got up in the morning my grandfather was on his knees beside the rocking chair in the living room. I would catch him on his knees. I found out later that he got up every morning at 4:30 to pray. And I can remember wanting to slip down to talk to my mother about a problem late at night and finding her on her knees. And it didn't matter how long I stayed, she was still going to be on her knees. I would have to slip back up to my room, come down early in the morning and catch her at her desk reading her Bible. It didn't matter what time I came down in the morning, she would be reading her Bible. I would catch them in prayer, catch them reading their Bible. Listen to me. When has your child caught you on your knees? When has your child caught you reading your Bible? When has your child caught you sharing the gospel with somebody? Do they see the reality of your faith, your love for Jesus, or is it just a show you put on for other people? Be real, phoniness will just quench the fire.

I can remember sharing the gospel with a German couple in South Africa. My daughter and I were down there to lead a conference. I have never run into such hostility against the gospel. The couple sliced me to shreds. I went back to my room that night and said, 'God, what have I done wrong. Did I use the wrong verse, the wrong tack?' And it came to me, maybe it wasn't for them, it was for my daughter. That she would hear me sharing the gospel and standing up for it even when I ran into such hostility. When have your children heard you personally sharing the gospel? I didn't just listen to my daddy in the pulpit. I listened to him in private and I've heard him sharing the gospel one on one. I've heard him praying, reading the Scriptures, and I've seen his heart for the gospel. He lives it and breaths it. It's not just something he puts on for the platform. No wonder he has passed the reality of his faith in Jesus to the next generation and the next generation. Now he's got great-grandchildren he's passing it to. Phoniness is a fire quencher.

There is something else the Lord said to me from this letter, and I just tuck it in for what it's worth: 'I know your deeds, you have a reputation for being alive, and you're dead.' The Lord has said that to me in the last twelve years. I was going around speaking everywhere and right from this letter He said, 'Ann, you have a reputation for being alive, a reputation for being a woman of the Word, but as I see you, you are dying.' Do you know why? Because I was prayerless. I wasn't spending time in prayer, I was just too tired. I have a prayer team, eight women at home who pray for me every day on their own and once a week together. They are praying for me during this message. Sometimes I will rely on their prayers instead of my own, I'll just spend time in the Word. I wasn't praying, I was prayerless. And the Lord said, 'You are shrivelling up because of prayerlessness.'

Is there somebody here who is prayerless? You used to spend time in prayer, not just going down your shopping list, but worshipping Him, praising Him, enjoying His presence, talking to Him about your day and letting Him know what was on your heart. He knows all of that, but when we come to Him in prayer like that we are developing a personal relationship with Him.

Prayerlessness and phoniness are fire quenchers. And so Jesus says, 'Listen to Me.' The principle is this: He is not fooled by our reputation, He looks on our heart and sees the reality of our faith and the fact that we are not passing it on, because perhaps we are hypocritical, or we are prayerless, and so He says, 'Listen to Me.' He has a promise for us in verse 5, 'He who overcomes will, like them, be dressed in white.' He will be right with God. 'I will never erase his name from the book of life, but will acknowledge his name before my father and his angels.' He is promising us a personal, permanent love relationship with Himself out of which stems everything in our Christian life. It's the heart beat, the well spring, the anchor, it is that which flows from us to our families, our neighbours and our churches. What is going to pass on our faith to the next generation is the reality of our love and our faith and our obedience and walk with Him which is real.

If you put on a mask, would you just drop it? You may say, 'I am scared for people to see me as I really am and to see the sin in my life and to see my struggles and my frailties. And I am not as spiritual as people think I am.' But if you drop the mask and begin to work at it, praying and spending time in your Bible and obeying, you are going to see that perhaps this week you lost your temper, next week you lose it less, next week you have victory over it and they're going to think – if God can help her to control her temper He can do the same for me. We begin to show each other the reality of the power of Christ. But how can people see that if we just go around pretending all the time? Would you be real and get on your knees, make time for prayer? I remember Dr Alan Redpath saying to an American audience, 'Do you know what American Christians need? They need blanket victory. Victory over those blankets in the morning, to get up and spend time on your knees in prayer.' I've prayed for blanket victory time and time again. I think I have been defeated more than I have been victorious; the victory for me is that I keep on trying, keep on getting up, keep on spending time with the Lord in prayer, that I would be real in my relationship with Him. Are you listening to what the Spirit is saying?

The church at Sardis was not listening to the Spirit. There's nothing but ruins there today.

6) The church at Philadelphia (Rev. 3:7–13)

There was no fire quencher in Philadelphia: they were doing everything right. Praise God, precious people – look forward to meeting them some day. I see a tendency in their lives to be timid in their service because they were afraid to walk through the open door, but they did.

7) The church at Laodicea (Rev. 3:14–22)

Here we see *the fire quencher of pride.* Jesus says, 'These are the words of the Amen, the faithful and true witness, the ruler of God's creation.' He begins by saying, 'Look at me. I am the truth.' The Laodiceans needed to look because, when He finishes with this letter, they are going to doubt what He was saying because it was so contrary to their view of themselves. He begins by saying, 'My words are true, listen to me. I am giving a faithful witness, learn from me. I know your deeds, I know what you are doing right – nothing.' There was not one thing in this church that was pleasing to God. 'I know what you are doing wrong – everything.' This is why everything was wrong. They were indifferent to Christ.

'I know your deeds, that you are neither cold nor hot. I wish you were either one or the other' (v. 15). If you were hot I could use you, if you were cold I could use you; I can't use something lukewarm. 'Because you are lukewarm – neither hot or cold – I am about to spit you out of my mouth.' They made Jesus sick. He wanted to use them for His kingdom and glory, to present the gospel to the world, but they were indifferent towards Him and He couldn't use them. Remember when He passed that fig tree on the way to Jerusalem with lots of leaves but no figs? And He cursed it, just like today, He gets angry when we have a leafy profession but no figs of real faith. And it's the same principle in John 15 when He purges the branch that does not bear fruit. He wants to use you and me. He wants us to be for His glory. He wants us to present the gospel to the world around us. He wants us to be conformed to the image of Christ. He wants us to be fruitful in our character and when we are not, it makes Him sick.

Then He says, 'Not only are you indifferent to me but you are ignorant of your condition. You say "I am rich [they thought they had eternal life]; I have acquired wealth and do not need a thing," but you do not realise you are wretched, pitiful, poor, blind and naked' (v. 17).

They had never even been born again. They had substituted a religion for a personal relationship with God. And so Jesus says, 'I counsel you to buy from me gold refined in the fire [buy from me real salvation] so you can become rich; and white clothes to wear [the righteousness of Christ] so you can cover your shameful nakedness; and salve [of the Holy Spirit] to put on your eyes so you can see [the truthfulness of your condition]' (v. 18).

I believe this is for somebody here, born and raised in the church, baptized as an infant, confirmed as a young adult. You take the sacraments, you go to church every Sunday, and you are involved as a deacon or an elder in leadership of the church, but you have never been born again. Nicodemus was the greatest religious leader in Israel. He was a household name. Everybody knew Nicodemus. He fasted three times a week, he knew the Scriptures inside and out, he kept the Law meticulously and he came to Jesus and said, 'Jesus, just tell me a little bit about heaven.' And Jesus looked at Nicodemus the great religious leader and said, 'You are never even going to see heaven, much less enter it, unless you are born again.' Religion doesn't make it. It doesn't matter how religious you are. You have to have a personal relationship with God through faith in Jesus Christ. The Laodiceans were so proud in their religion, their traditions, their ritual, their church denomination, that they had never humbled themselves, confessing they were sinners, at the foot of the cross, repenting of their sin and receiving Christ as their Saviour. Jesus says, in verse 19, 'Those whom I love I rebuke and discipline.' The Lord loves the Laodiceans and you, whoever you are – proud, religious person steeped in ritual and tradition. The Lord God has drawn you to Keswick this week to tell you that He loves you, but He counsels you to be born again, to repent of your pride.

Verse 20 is so familiar, isn't it? It was given to the church – to religious people. 'Behold, I stand at the door and knock.' He was on the outside of the church, locked out, knocking to be let in. Is He locked out of your heart? Why? Maybe there is a deep grievance in your life, anger towards God because of something He has allowed, a suffering, an injustice, an abuse. Maybe there is unforgiveness towards someone and you have locked your heart; it's tight and it's hard. Whatever it is, He says, 'I'm knocking at your heart's door and if you will open the door I will come in and sup with you.' That's a promise of fellowship with the living God. Knowing Him in a personal love relationship. Are you listening to what the Spirit is saying? The principle is this: 'You must be born again.' That's not a Baptist thing, or a 'Billy Graham Evangelistic Crusade' thing, that's what Jesus says: John 3, 'You must be born again.' It's not an option. If you want to go to heaven, if you want to receive eternal life, if you want to be right with God, YOU MUST BE BORN AGAIN.

And the promise is this:'To the one who overcomes I will give the right to sit with me on my throne, just as I overcame and sat down with My Father on his throne' (v. 21). In other words, I am going to give you the right to be accepted in heaven. You will be as accepted in heaven as Jesus is. Can you imagine that? It doesn't matter who you are or what you have done; when you come to the cross by faith and you confess your sin and you repent and you receive Him into your life, you are washed clean of your sin, you are clothed in the righteousness of Christ. Heaven's door opens and you are as welcome as Jesus is. Now that's a promise. Are you listening to what the Spirit is saying?

Pride is a fire quencher. The church at Laodicea refused to listen. There is no church there today. So my challenge to you is to examine your heart and your life for the fire quenchers – things that put the fire out. Bring them to the cross and confess them as the sin they are. Repent and ask God to help you. I believe God will light the fire and by the time you leave here you are going to be on fire. God willing, the fire will spread and maybe, once again, in our day, we will have revival. Would you listen to what the Spirit is saying?

Priorities for Followers
by Luis Palau

Luke 10:1–41

This is only my second time at Keswick and the Lord has touched my soul in a special way.

On this closing night we realize that during the week the Lord has spoken to us about solid biblical doctrine, about guilt and sin, cleansing and rededication. We've had a great emphasis on outreach and mission, the Lordship of Christ, the church and all its value and beauty. Tonight we want to close with a call to look forward. Keswick, now in its 125th year, arose for a very special reason and purpose during the days when there was a great harvest in the UK and many coming to Christ, as you read in *Transforming Keswick*. D.L. Moody was having campaigns and thousands were being converted to Jesus Christ. One campaign in London lasted nine months. There were three services every night, no Underground, no cars, just mud and horse-drawn carriages. What a campaign! But things have changed. I'd give my life to have a nine-month campaign. But nobody wants it, so you have to take what you can get as an evangelist! But in those days, it happened because there were so many believers who knew Jesus as Saviour but didn't know how to enjoy their daily life.

I was like that until at the age of twenty-five, I heard Major

Ian Thomas of the Torchbearers speak at my Bible College. He spoke for twenty-two minutes on Moses and the burning bush and everything I have read about Keswick all came together. I knew sin must be got rid of by the cleansing of the blood, and we must rededicate our bodies as a gift to the Lord (Rom. 12:1), but the thing that was missing was the indwelling life of the resurrected Lord Jesus, and how that actually worked. I couldn't get it. I used to think 'I stand at the door and knock' was figurative. Isn't that strange? I couldn't quite understand that if Jesus is seated at the right hand of the Father, how can He be here at the same time?

I was really hungry and felt something was horribly missing in my life. There was joy in the gospel. I was saved. I knew I was going to heaven. Jesus was my Saviour, no question about that. But in between salvation and heaven there seemed to be a massive lack, and Ian Thomas went straight to Moses and the burning bush. I'll tell you a little bit about it later.

Now we are going to look at three things in Luke 10 and then I want to call you, in the name of Jesus Christ, to a renewal of your vows. All of us can look back to a time when God dealt with us in depth, but we cannot spend our lives talking about 'when I was twenty-five'. I cannot live on the experiences of 1960, I've got to live in this year 2000. Look at Luke 9:62: 'Jesus replied, "No one who puts his hand to the plough and looks back is fit for service in the kingdom of God."' That is the *past* – looking back. Now let's read a verse about the *present* and our awesome union with Jesus Christ. Luke 10:16, 'He who listens to you listens to me; He who rejects you rejects me; but he who rejects me rejects Him who sent me.' Then Luke 10:42 – the *future*: ' "Mary has chosen what is better and it will not be taken away from her." '

To put it all together, turn to John 7:37–39:

On the last [like today] and greatest day of the Feast, Jesus stood and said in a loud voice; 'If any man is thirsty, let him come to me and drink. Whoever believes in me, as the Scripture has said, streams of living water will flow from within him.' By this he meant the Spirit, whom those who believed in him were later to receive. Up to that time the Spirit had not been given, since Jesus had not been glorified.

And lastly, John 16:20–24:

> I tell you the truth, you will weep and mourn while the world
> rejoices. You will grieve, but your grief will turn to joy. A
> woman giving birth to a child has pain because her time has
> come; but when her baby is born she forgets the anguish be-
> cause of her joy that a child is born into the world. So with
> you: Now is your time of grief, but I will see you again and
> you will rejoice, and no one will take away your joy. In that
> day you will no longer ask me anything. I tell you the truth,
> my Father will give you whatever you ask in my name. Until
> now you have not asked for anything in my name. Ask and
> you will receive, and your joy will be complete.

Before we go back to Luke, just look at this passage. I have
underlined in my Bible three major times when it says Joy, Joy,
Joy. At the Children's Special Service Mission we used to sing,
'Joy, joy, joy, with joy my heart is ringing, With joy I will carry
on,' and it was very meaningful. I wanted to point to verse 20,
'You will grieve, [because of the crucifixion and burial], but
your grief will turn to joy.' Jesus is alive! And verse 22b, 'But I
will see you again [I think this is the resurrection but it implies
the Second Coming], and you will rejoice, and no one will
take away your joy.' And finally the climax of joy, 'Ask and you
will receive and your joy will be – what? COMPLETE!' Are
you rejoicing?

I remember a black singer in America asked, 'How many of
you are rejoicing in the Lord tonight?' and most hands went
up. Then he said, 'Would you mind informing your face?'
Some people honestly think that enjoying life is somehow
unspiritual. That is very hard to believe. In this passage alone
the Lord says, joy, joy, joy – three times. My sins are forgiven –
every one of them. I have the Holy Spirit. I'm going to heaven
when I die. I have got good reason to rejoice just a tiny bit!
Christianity has intellectual content, but also there is rejoicing;
don't be afraid to rejoice.

However, not everyone rejoices and it is no use kidding
yourself. You can't pump it up. After a while you feel you
don't want to be a hypocrite. You aren't going to put on a
show for the benefit of others, you aren't happy, so you will

look miserable. We've all gone through that, so let's look at Luke 9:62.

The past

You must make a full break with the past. This week I have made a full break with certain things, in my not-too-distant past, that needed to be left behind. That's why I'll always remember Keswick 2000. Look at what He says, 'No one who puts his hand to the plough and looks back is fit for service [fit for heaven, by the blood of Christ, but not fit for service] in the kingdom of God.' Leave the past behind. When Christ was crucified we were crucified with Him. It's a mystery, but it's true. When Christ was buried we were buried with Him. When Christ rose we rose with Him.

How do we leave our past behind? Our memories don't shut off immediately, but it is amazing how the Lord can help us to erase memories if we ask Him to. The Bible says that when we understand that we died with Christ, to sin, to the world and to Satan, it doesn't mean that the world, sin and Satan have disappeared from the scene, but that we have made a cut-off from them. And when we are buried with Christ it means that we can leave things behind, because we are now risen with Him. Goodbye past! 'Therefore, if anyone is in Christ, he is a new person altogether; the old has passed the new has come!' (cf. 2 Cor. 5:17)

Don't become obsessed with generational curses. I don't believe they existed and the Bible says, 'A curse without a cause will not alight' (Prov. 26:2 AV). Nobody who cursed your great-grandpa in the fourteenth century is going to catch up with you in this century. You are a new Christian in Jesus Christ. You are born again. Did you bury the past? Satan would like us to believe that he can curse our great-grandpa and reach out to us, just to keep us in fear. Real love casts out fear. Bury the past; even if there were curses, they are gone, they cannot touch you.

Leave personal failures behind, the blood of Jesus Christ cleanses from all sin. Some of you have made sad and wrong decisions, but leave them behind. 'No one who puts his hand to the plough and looks back is worthy of service in the kingdom of God.' If you keep looking back you will lose your joy: If you lose your joy, you are not going to be fruitful. If you are not fruitful you are not going to see blessing through you. When you put your hand to the plough, you mean business with Jesus Christ, you are connected with Him. Don't look back: the past is forgiven. Buried with Christ, you are risen with Christ. You can begin again. We see in 1 Corinthians 4 that we are the scum of the earth, and some of you feel like you are the scum of the earth, not because somebody else has pushed you, but because of something you did. Tonight you can bow before the Saviour, renew your vows and bury the past, leaving it behind. Don't keep digging up your cadaver, leave it in the grave. It's in the past; you are forgiven, you are alive in Jesus Christ.

Today I talked with a man who was divorced. He took responsibility for that. His daughter is in a real state of rebellion, with a child out of wedlock, and his son is doing little better. He is confused and searching for God's guidance and he said to me, 'Luis, I fear that I have missed the boat.' I want to tell you, 'There is another boat coming at 9 o'clock.' If you have missed the boat, you can get on the next one. You don't have to beat yourself over the head forever. Yes, divorcing your wife and leaving your children was not right and that is why perhaps you are in pain because your girl got angry and started messing around and got pregnant, all that hurts.

You cannot live in the past forever, you have to come to the cross. The beauty of the cross is that you can finish with this thing once and for all and break with it. Jesus doesn't want to berate us for the rest of our days. The Holy Spirit convicts of sin and then, when we repent and are forgiven, it's over. You may remember, your mother-in-law may remember, but the Lord says, 'Your sins and evil deeds, I will remember no more' (cf. Jer. 31:34). You missed the first boat, there's a second boat coming. You have the chance to get on again.

The apostle Paul often went through experiences that

reminded him of the bad old days. In 2 Corinthians 1:4, he is talking about going into Ephesus where they stoned him and they thought they had left him for dead, and he says in 2 Corinthians 1:9, 'Indeed, in our hearts we felt the sentence of death. But this happened that we might not rely on ourselves but on God, who raises the dead.' God is the God who raises the dead. If you feel you haven't just messed up to here, but are under the mud and the mire, then you are a candidate for the God who raises the dead. If you've reached the end of your tether, you may feel, that's it, the Lord's had it with me. I was raised up in a Brethren assembly and knew the Bible before I went to school, and now look at me. I was brought up in the Anglican Church, I knew all the prayers, I did communion, and look at what I've done now: the Lord's finished with me. In a sense He has not finished with you; He has finished with the old side of you.

Come to the God who raises the dead. He is here tonight and He says, 'My boy, I want you back. I don't want you sitting in the dark, sad and lonely and feeling rejected or rejecting yourself for service.' Leave it behind, look forward. If you want to do a straight furrow you have to keep your eyes up on the horizon. If you turn around, the oxen will start messing around. To keep a straight row keep your eyes up front, that is what the Holy Spirit is saying. Some people seem to relish their stupid sins, pardon the expression. Don't look back on them. What are you trying to do? Re-cook them! Remember them! The Lord says, 'Don't look back.' Don't dig up the past – rejoice, and let the joy of the Lord show in your life.

Now, the God who raises the dead, what are we supposed to do about it? The teaching of Keswick is that the Christian life is a crisis and a process. A crisis happens the first time you understand the risen, resurrected Lord Jesus living in you. And the crisis may come again if you forget the risen Lord Jesus living in you and have a major stumble, like some of us have had through the years. And then you have got to come back almost as if you had never learned the lesson in the first place – another crisis. But there is a process. The Holy Spirit has said to you, 'You've been faithful to the doctrine, you are strong on John 3:16, you carry your Bible and

you mean business, but you've lost the joy of the Lord.'
How about allowing the living Christ to fill you again and
rejoice again and live again?

The Lord says, 'Joy, joy, joy.' Rejoice that your names are
written in heaven. So what is the step? Consider before the
Lord if you have drifted away, if you are not as joyful as you
used to be when you were younger. You have become listless
and un-joyful. When young people look at you they say,
'When I hit seventy, I sure don't want to look like him!' If you
have become that type of person, you're not joyful, you are
sinning. What is clogging your joy?

The present

'He who listens to you listens to me; he who rejects you
rejects me; but he who rejects me rejects Him who sent me'
(Lk. 10:16). I call this an awesome union. If somebody rejects
you when you speak, filled with the Spirit under the control
of the indwelling Christ, they are rejecting Jesus Christ. If they
listen to you, they are listening to Jesus Christ, and not only
Him but the Father who sent Him. What an awesome union!
We are not little ants crawling around the world doing our
best for Jesus, sweating as much as we can to do the best for
the kingdom. Rolling up our sleeves and showing the Lord,
'Man! I really love you. You know I love you. You got somebody great when you got me. Lord, I'm really going to win
the world!' I used to think that. After a while you run out of
petrol and you begin to say, 'I've had it. I'm worn out, I'm
exhausted.' To be tired is one thing, to be exhausted is another.
When you are tired, eight hours of sleep, and you bounce
back. Exhaustion is trying to serve the kingdom in the
strength of the flesh. And it was never meant to be that way.

Listen to some quotations that all of you know off by heart.
Galatians 2:20: 'I have been crucified with Christ and I no
longer live, but Christ lives in me. The life I live in the body, I
live by faith in the Son of God, who loved me and gave himself for me.' God used Ian Thomas to speak this and to shatter
my soul. Luis, Christ lives in me. Not figuratively, not perhaps,

not as a beautiful thought – He literally lives in me. That is the secret of the awesome union with God Almighty.

Second verse, Ephesians 3:19: 'That you may be filled to the measure of all the fullness of God.' We will never achieve it a hundred per cent until we get to heaven where we shall be like Him, because we shall see Him as He is. But the goal is still that we should be filled to all the fullness of God. That is not just hot air that the apostle Paul thought up. What he says is inspired by the Holy Spirit: 'I pray that you may know the love of God so that you can be filled to all the fullness of God.'

Remember Psalm 23:5. 'Anoint my head with oil, my cup [AV is the best translation] runneth over.' And you know a true walk with God when you understand that the union with the living Christ is not something you create, it is a fact. It is something you understand, accept and begin to act upon. Christ lives in me. You anoint my head with oil, the Holy Spirit. My cup runneth over. When I have been at my best, in my walk with Christ, I know the cup runneth over. You feel it spilling all around. You know other people have been blessed. Is your cup running over? It's a deep question. You can know a lot of Bible and your cup not be running over. You could be checking out John Stott and your cup not be running over. You can spit out doctrine perfectly and yet your cup not be running over. Your mind may be filled with knowledge, but your spirit and your soul can be on their own. And the Scripture teaches this awesome union. That is what Keswick was really all about, to remind God's people: not only is the past forgiven, not only when you die are you going to heaven – glorious truths, but between then and then is the fullness of the indwelling Christ, Amen!

In John 7 the Lord says, 'If anyone is thirsty let him come to me and drink.' If you are not a joyful Christian you should be and you cannot blame anybody but yourself. You cannot blame your spouse, even if they are mean and abrupt; you cannot blame your mother-in-law, no matter who she may be. It is an easy thing to blame the elders, to blame the preacher, to blame church history, to blame our style, to blame the music or the lack of music, or the modern music, or the boring music, or whatever. You blame someone else and you will end up a miserable Christian. It is so unnecessary. Some people actually like it. I don't and the Lord doesn't want us to.

Recently I was giving an interview and I asked the newswoman if the convention bugs the locals. She said, 'Don't pay too much attention. Tell them over there not to worry. Because the bed and breakfasts and restaurants are full, they are not complaining that much.' She went on, 'I must say something though. I was walking my 6-year-old grandson along the pavement the other day and two ladies from your group came and they looked like they could kill the little boy because I didn't pull him off the pavement.' I said, 'They couldn't have been from the convention because our people are wonderful.' She said, 'Well these two were.' I said, 'How do you know?' She said, 'They had two of those big Bibles.' I said, 'Are you sure?' She said, 'I'm sure.' I don't know who the two ladies were, but they looked at the child as if they could kill him, because he wasn't getting out of their way.

If you are not a happy Christian there's something really wrong with you. Don't you think that's spirituality or that's the way your denomination does it, or that you were born that way. Because the Lord came and said the fruit of the Spirit is love, is *joy*. Some people say, 'Well, I can have joy without looking like it.' I don't believe that at all. There is no distinction between joy and happiness. If you are happy, it is because you have joy, and if you do not have joy, you are not going to be happy. Are you joyful in Jesus Christ? Or are you a sour Christian? Don't just say, 'I don't like Palau – why do they bring Argentines?' You don't have to like me, but I am here to speak to you in the name of the Lord. England needs spirit-controlled Christians, so does America and Argentina, but we are in England now.

You may feel you can't work it out. That's how I felt until I heard Ian Thomas, who put it this way with a great illustration. Moses thought he could do it on his own. He was born in the right family, adopted by the daughter of the Pharaoh, educated in the best university, he had the right connections, the right everything, and he thought, 'My time has come to liberate Israel.' So he walks out in the fire of the flesh and the first thing he does – he kills an Egyptian, then he buries him. The next day two Jews are fighting, he exorts them, they say to him, 'You're going to kill us too.' He runs off. The fire of the flesh lasted thirty-six hours. Seven girls save his skin and take him to their dad.

Forty years – nothing happening. When he walked down the pavement he looked at the children. 'Get out of my way!' He was in the desert for forty years. And then God appears to him in a most unusual way, a bunch of sticks start burning, but they don't get consumed and Moses says, 'I am going to see what this is.' He gets near. God says, 'Moses, take off your shoes. This is holy ground.' You know the story. Ian Thomas gave an application that revolutionized me. I need it again tonight. It was this: 'Moses, you thought that I wanted an educated bush, a pretty bush, a well-connected bush, but Moses, any old bush will do as long as God is in the bush.' And Moses got it and the following forty years were the most fruitful of his entire life.

The divorced man who talked with me today is forty-seven and I said to him, 'You've got more than a third of your life left to go.' Moses had a third of his life filled with the spirit, fruitful, powerful. If you are here tonight and you forgot that Jesus is alive, you forgot that He dwells in you, you forgot that He has all the power you need, before we go to communion come to Him and the Lord will give you confidence and authority. That isn't yours by education, personality, connections, training, experience, savvy, having a high I.Q. That is all useful, but that is not the power; the power is that the living Christ lives within you and I am crucified with Christ. And Jesus says in the last prayer in John 17, 'Father… I in them and you in me. May they be brought to complete unity to let the world know that you sent me…' The union with God the Father was in Jesus. Jesus is in us and he who receives you, receives Me and he who rejects you, rejects Me and the one who sent Me. That is an awesome union. That is what Keswick is meant to bring each one of us. 'Whoever unites or joins himself with the Lord becomes one spirit with Him' (1 Cor. 6:17).

I needed this week to be reminded of these fundamentals. If you have been looking back, leave it, bury it – all is forgiven. If you forgot that the indwelling Lord Jesus was in you, don't be surprised. We all forget. That's why once in a while you hear of a well-known preacher who has a major fall. We all forget. We can carry on with our ministry, we get excited about the opportunities and God uses us, but we haven't realized it, we have forgotten the fundamentals. Every morning when we get up we should say, 'Thank you Lord Jesus. You're alive, You dwell in me, all the fullness of God dwells in me in bodily form – I am complete in Jesus Christ. Thank you Lord, today temptations will come, but your power is sufficient. There will be opportunities to witness – I'm not very gifted, but you are wise. I will be tempted, but I will overcome because you are here. Thank you. I haven't forgotten.' Keswick is all about reminding us that we are the temple of the living God.

The future

Look at Mary and remember she chose to sit at the feet of Jesus. I call this 'intentional intimacy'. Psalm 25:14 says, 'The Lord confides in those who fear him; he makes his covenant known to them.' My pastor once said, 'God has no favourites but He does have intimates.' And the intimates are those who intentionally get close to Him, who intentionally near Him. If you love Him today, and if you really have forgotten about the indwelling Christ, it may be good to take a moment of silence, before we remember the cross and the resurrection of the Master. Take a moment and say, 'Lord Jesus, I intentionally want to leave the past behind. Lord Jesus, thank you for reminding me that it's not I, but Christ in me. Any old bush will do as long as God is in the bush. I can stay close to you, so that you can reveal your covenant to me.'

Upside-down Kingdom
by Derek Tidball

Luke 14

A friend of mine, a Bible College principal, had to welcome his local bishop to preach in the college chapel. He'd always been irritated by his pomposity. So as he greeted the bishop he took him into a side room and said, 'If you'll excuse me a moment, my Lord, I'll leave you here. I am going to collect your chauffeur and take him into the chapel.' The Bishop was left stranded, while his chauffeur was conducted into a seat of honour in the college chapel. My friend then went back to pray with the Bishop and conduct him into worship. How do you react to that action of my friend? Was he being rude and disrespectful? Was he wrongly being irritated by what he regarded as pompous behaviour earlier? Was he acting out of a sense of political correctness? Or was he being Christ-like? Judge your reaction according to Luke 14.

Luke leads us into the strange world of the *upside-down kingdom* – the kingdom of God, which, to quote Alice in Wonderland, makes it seem 'quite dull and stupid for life to go on in the common way'. During a conversation at a Sabbath lunch, around a dining room table, Jesus introduces a profoundly out-of-the-ordinary challenge to us today. As one commentator says, 'For Luke there is nothing more important that a dining room table.' Jesus is always teaching over a meal. And you can understand why: the dining room table is the place where we learn a lot. Remember mum saying, 'Get your elbows off the table.' Many things are taught there, but it's also the place of friendship, the place of intimacy. It's the place where you learn and where you let your guard down. While the conversation drifts you reveal what you really trust in and believe in. And in the argy-bargy of any family, it's there that arguments take place and the rough edges get smoothed off. It's not suprising that so much of Jesus' ministry took place around the meal table. And in the space of twenty-four verses, in Luke 14, Jesus introduces us to four great values of the kingdom of God which are profoundly upside-down values. They were then and I guarantee, for most evangelical churches, they still are today.

1) The kingdom of God is about healing the untouchable (14:1–6)

Luke 14:1–6 tells of the meal, which begins somewhat uneasily. The small talk is just getting off the ground and they are wondering how to handle this visiting Rabbi – Jesus, who had undoubtedly just spoken in the synagogue and been invited home to Sabbath lunch, as would be the custom of the day. But the conversation doesn't get very far before it's rudely interrupted by the arrival of a man with dropsy. Jesus now faces three challenges:

a) The challenge of the context

It's happening on the Sabbath in the house of a prominent Pharisee and He is being watched and tested, not on whether he can use His knife and fork correctly but, more significantly, on His attitudes. How was He going to handle Himself? What would He say about the Law? The atmosphere was suspicious and icy, as it often is over a Sunday lunch when the preacher rather than the joint is dissected! That was the context in which Jesus was about to minister. With the interruption came a second challenge:

b) The challenge of the sick man

There in front of Him, verse 2, was a man suffering from dropsy. How inconvenient and embarrassing in polite social company. How did this man with dropsy get in, unless it was a set-up, which it might have been? He was unlikely to have got in by any legitimate means. Perhaps he was gate crashing. Do you understand the significance of the man with dropsy? It wasn't just that his swollen body wasn't a pretty sight. More significant was the fact that somebody unclean coming into the meal would render the whole meal contaminated and defiled. The Pharisees, and it was a prominent Pharisee's house in which they were meeting, would have had to go through ritual cleansing before they could enjoy the meal. I suspect it was a set-up, to see how Jesus would handle this situation. And if the context and the interruption were not enough, Jesus also faced:

c) The challenge of the Sabbath

It was, verses 3–4, the Sabbath day. Was healing work? And if it was work, should you do it on the Sabbath? What do you do when you are presented with someone with dropsy and you have the power to heal them? Jesus points out to them that though He is the 'Lord of the Sabbath' (Lk. 6:5), He never subverts the Law. He cuts through the conventional interpretations of the Law which tie people in knots. Their hope of trapping Him fails. He has turned the tables.

These first six verses not only speak about the challenge Jesus faces, but also the challenge that Jesus issues. Confronted with this sick person, He engages in a liberating act. He takes hold of the man, heals him and sends him away. He touches the unclean person. He doesn't do that like Princess Diana used to with Aids victims. Oh, there was worth and value in what she did; her touch gave them emotional support and human dignity and that is good. But Jesus is risking contamination as He, the holy, clean One, touches this sick, defiled, unclean individual. He doesn't just express love or emotional support or dignity, but heals him.

Luke chooses a very interesting word to express the healing. He talks about Jesus 'liberating' him, setting him free. The

kingdom of God is about liberating those who are enslaved
through the saving act of Jesus, through the healing touch of
Jesus. But then Jesus drives the point home. He not only challenges them by His liberating act but by His liberating proclamation, His liberating law. The act is explained in verse 5 by a
discussion of what the Law means. Even the legalistic Pharisees, He points out, would accept that if a child or animal fell
into a pit on the Sabbath, they could be rescued. But what
about this man? Jesus' irresistible logic says that, if it is permitted to save a child and rescue an animal, is not the healing of
an adult worth more?

The Sabbath is not a time for rules and regulations and
legalism and judging whether it is legitimate to do this or not.
The kingdom principle is a principle of healing and liberating.
Jesus had already spoken in His own synagogue in Nazareth
about the Jubilee having appeared, the time of liberation (Lk.
4). Now in this prominent Pharisee's house, over the Sabbath
lunch table, He puts that liberation into action.

In this chapter, every time Jesus makes a new point, He holds
up a mirror to those who are listening, showing them and us
something of the sin that lurks within our own hearts. Here,
He is pointing out the sin of hard-heartedness. He holds up the
mirror to us to question whether we, like those people at the
meal, are suspicious of Jesus, are always trying to test Him out.
Whether we will follow Jesus as Lord – providing He confirms
our rules and regulations and lives up to our expectations. Providing He doesn't do anything terribly suprising or terribly
upsetting. Providing He is very well-behaved in the church to
which we belong. Many of us are hard hearted – not wanting
to hear the genuine Word of Jesus, testing Him out all the time,
giving Him a tick for this and a cross for that and weighing up
whether He is worth following or not.

2) The kingdom of God is about doing the unreasonable (14:7–11)

Luke writes with a delicious sense of irony. He begins the
chapter by saying, 'They were watching Him.' But then,

verse 7, 'When He noticed how the guests picked the places of honour at the table, He told them this parable.' They may indeed have been watching Him, but the truth of the matter was that He was watching them, and He comments on their normal, routine behaviour – the way we all behave in our everyday life. Normally we go for the place of honour; we go for the best seats; we jockey for position and recognition; we protect our own rights; we want to be known by others. Like the parents at my son's school play, making sure they got the best seats at the front because their little Johnny was going to do something totally remarkable. Being British, we know our rights. When someone pushes into the bus queue or the supermarket line, we know we were next in line! We save our seats here in the convention tent! What Jesus is pointing out is nothing unusual, it still goes on, doesn't it? It's the normal social, conventional behaviour.

Therefore, to them and to us, Jesus said, being a kingdom person is about 'doing the unreasonable'. Set aside the normal, social, conventional behaviour. Instead adopt the radical kingdom perspective, which is, verse 10, to take the lowest place genuinely, with integrity. Not with our ears cocked to the high table, like a dog has its ear cocked ready for walkies, waiting for the call, 'Come up higher.' It's not a nice strategy that makes us appear humble while all the time we are angling for a seat at the top. Don Cranebill says:

> The normal tendency is to chase after positions of honour and prestige. We all enjoy the 'oohs and the ahs' of other people. We take it for granted that upward is better. Rather than endorsing such upward mobility Jesus calls us to downward mobility, to the seat at the bottom. His disciples defer to others. They happily yield up the good seats. In fact they are so busy waiting on tables that they don't have time to sit down. Serving is their occupation not seat picking.

Will you remember that, next Sunday morning when, back in your church, someone is sitting in your favourite seat? We laugh, but this is the measure of kingdom behaviour, isn't it? This is how radical it is. How do we measure up to Jesus' words, or should I say, how do we measure down to Jesus' words?

If the mirror, in the first incident, pointed out the sin of hard-heartedness, the mirror is held up on this occasion to point out the sin of pride. And I think nobody has written about it personally and analysed it more brilliantly in recent days than Jonathan Aitken, the former cabinet minister. In his very moving book, *Pride and Perjury*, Jonathan Aitken speaks of the exultation of power, the exhilaration of being in control, of his cup overflowing when at long last, after many years in Parliament, John Major invited him to join the government and have a seat at the Cabinet table. You will know the story: how from that position of eminence, very swiftly, because of a lie, Jonathan Aitken found himself not only out of office, but out of Parliament and out of home and out of liberty as he served a jail sentence for perjury. When he went to tell his son at Eton that he was likely to face a jail sentence, his son asked him what had gone wrong. Jonathan Aitken replied, 'I have made the greatest mistake of my life, because I have been proud, arrogant, blind and dishonest. Now I am going to have to pay a heavy price for those sins, for that is what they are.' He goes on to quote C.S. Lewis, 'There is one vice from which no one in the world is free, the vice that I am talking about is that of pride.'

Pride leads to every other vice; it is the complete anti-God state of mind. It is a spiritual cancer, and it is shown in the ordinary little acts: sitting around a dining room table; pushing for a seat. We are too well mannered, too well brought up and too evangelical to let it show too much. We can control it when the issue is big, when we think other people are watching, but it's the ordinary little acts that betray the pride.

3) The kingdom of God is about inviting the undesirable (14:12-14)

From looking at the guests, Jesus now turns His fire on the hosts, who up to now would have been rather glad about what Jesus has said. 'That's right Jesus, you tell them.' It would be easier to have a dinner party if people didn't all want to sit in the best positions; it would make being a host much easier. I reckon they were pretty relaxed up to this point. But Jesus soon wipes the smiles off their faces, as He talks again about socially conventional behaviour. This time not of the guest, but of the host (v. 12). When you are going to host a banquet, or an ordinary Sabbath lunch, who do you invite? Most people invite those who are naturally close to them, friends, relatives. Of course they also invite rich neighbours – people who are significant, people who can invite you back. You invite people who will make you feel good because they like you or make you look good, because they are people of standing.

This was well-known behaviour of the day. In Jewish society, you didn't invite people who were beneath your standing, but those of equal standing or above, because they would give you prestige and further honour. Just like they do at Hollywood parties. We grade people according to their usefulness to us. But the kingdom is an upside-down kingdom. And instead of socially conventional behaviour, we ought to be people who engage in spiritually intentional behaviour, which is so radically different.

The kingdom principle is to invite those who would never be able to invite us back. Luke lists them here: the poor, the crippled, the lame and the blind. Those who aren't in a position to repay you. That list is also found in Luke 4:16–30, echoing the Magnificat that Mary sang, recorded in Luke 1:46 onwards. The kingdom turning everything on its head is a recurring theme in Luke's Gospel. The rich, the powerful and the well fed are dethroned from their positions, while those who are poor, hungry and of no social standing are lifted up.

Here is sheer grace in operation: giving without strings attached. This is not the ugly face of generosity that gives in order to control and to exercise power over people, as governments do in so-called 'helping' Third World countries. This is just free giving without any return expected. Giving to an unreasonable degree. That is irrational according to any market economy and makes no sense in a capitalist economy. Giving for the sheer joy of giving leads, says Jesus in verse 14, to a state of blessedness. If you want to be blessed, then God will do it when you invite the poor, the crippled, the lame and the blind. Maybe one of the reasons why there isn't any blessing in many of our churches is not because we don't desire it and we are not intense in our prayer for it, but because we are just not putting into operation the plain, ordinary teaching of Jesus in an obedient fashion.

These were the people, the poor and the blind and the lame who, according to all the indices of the day, were excluded people. They didn't have a place amongst the people of God, but kingdom disciples include them, not by sending them a donation, or supporting a charity whose work is with the poor, but by inviting them and by sitting down at table with them – by having a relationship with them. When I was last in pastoral ministry the most effective thing my wife and I ever did, beyond all my preaching, was to take a 26-year-old lad into our care on bail from the courts. The feedback we got showed that that one simple act had more impact for the gospel of Christ than all the sermons I had ever preached. We were actually doing what Jesus told us we should do.

So who do you send your Christmas cards to? Those you receive them from or those you never expect to hear from? Who do you invite to Sunday lunch? Those who will invite you back next Sunday? Who do you have to stay with you? Criminals, the socially feeble, the poor, the despised, the oddballs, those who don't fit in, the ethnic minorities, the alcoholics, the people who are struggling to make it in life, or the people who are well set up like you?

The mirror held up here reveals the sin of 'ungrace' as Philip Yancey in that marvellous book, *What's So Amazing About Grace?* calls it. He describes how from nursery school onwards we are taught to succeed in a world of ungrace, 'The early bird gets the worm.' 'There is no such thing as a free lunch.' 'Demand your rights.' 'Get what you pay for.' I know these rules work well, he says, for I have lived by them. I work for what I earn. I like to win. I insist on my own rights. I want people to get what they deserve – nothing more, nothing less. That is how we carry on in many of our churches and it raises the question as to whether we have understood grace. For if God's grace has flown into our lives, then it should turn us upside down and we, in grace, should flow out with love into the lives of others.

4) The kingdom of God is about thinking the unimaginable (14:15–23)

Jesus wraps this incident up by moving on to a different plane. From observing particular social behaviour, He gives a grand spiritual vision and tells us about the way in which God is going to work at the end of all things. There is a problem in verse 15 that Jesus addresses. One of the guests, who is obviously having a good time, is confident of a seat at the table of the Messiah's banquet at the end of the age: the banquet that was envisaged by Abraham and spoken of in Isaiah 25, when God reigns and everything in creation would be summed up. Jesus tells a story about a party to answer the problem of just who will be at that banquet. Verses 16–17 leave us in no doubt that this party was going to be the place to be seen, determining who was 'in' and who was 'out'. It was going to be, says Luke, 'a great banquet', not just a meal at the local chippy, but a magnificent spread. There would be many guests, not just a few. Everybody would know about this one. The preparation was going to be well done. They used the system of double invitations as No. 10 Downing Street or Buckingham Palace do today. If you ever get an invitation from the Queen, you will be asked, first of all, if you will accept it, before you are issued it. She does not wish to be turned down. They will contact you and say, 'If Her Majesty were to … would you be free?' Well, that's the system that operated here. So these people, who eventually turned down the prominent landowner, the party giver, are more culpable that they appear in our translation. They have already been 'sussed out' as to whether they are available or not.

Look at the suprising plot that Jesus unfolds in verses 18–20. The expected guests reject His invitation. Those who have already said, 'I'll be free on the night, I'll be there,' suddenly come up with the most suprising of excuses. No property would ever have been bought by a Jew without being checked out first. To say to the host, 'Well, I've just bought a field and I must go and see it, please excuse me,' must be a downright lie. And no oxen would be bought, especially five yoke of oxen (the number suggests this was a prominent land-owner), without being tested first. Buy them and then road-test them! No bride (if the women will forgive me, this a social comment about the world as it was) would have been allowed to stand in the way of an invitation like this. She wasn't worth that much in the ancient world. So it's no wonder that the host, Jesus tells us, is angry. This is a deliberate slight which says this party-giver is of no value. He doesn't matter. He isn't where the action is.

The plot continues to unravel with the unexpected guests being invited and accepting. Two categories of guests are now included in the invitation: those who lived in the town and were unfit – the poor, the crippled, the blind and the lame; and now those who live outside the city and are homeless. 'Make them come in,' says the host. Not because he is an advocate of muscular Christianity, but the text recognizes that such people would find it hard to believe that such an invitation was genuine. Jesus is saying, it's not the expected, the conventional, the respectable people who will be found at the Messiah's banquet. This is a banquet of grace and love, which has been undeserved, but which has been accepted in faith by the undeserving. It is for the unworthy.

This holds up a mirror to us, doesn't it? We have to say that we are the people who might expect to be at the Messiah's banquet. You would expect to find the Baptist deacon there, the Anglican church warden, the PCC member, the Brethren elder, the Bible College lecturer, the Keswick-goer. So here is a terrifying word from Jesus. His kingdom is so upside down we need to make sure that we don't reject the invitation to be at the Messiah's banquet. Not by saying, 'No,' but by disobeying Him in the way in which we live.

Around the table, Jesus exposes the sin of hard-heartedness, the sin of pride, the sin of un-grace, the sin of disobedience and rejection. And He turns all our conventional behaviour, then and now, on its head, telling us that the kingdom operates in an entirely different way. We need to be the people in

Britain today who are concerned about exclusion, who embrace the untouchable, do the unthinkable, invite the undesirable and think the unimaginable. That's true holiness. Not being concerned, as the Pharisees were, about personal purity and ritual piety, but about a social engagement that transforms the world in which we live because it challenges socially conventional behaviour. Not being 'holier than thou', and condemning it prophetically and speaking down to it. But challenging it precisely because we are the people who do touch the untouchable and embrace and invite the undesirable, who take the lowest places and think the unthinkable and believe that God's kingdom won't be measured by the way in which the normal kingdoms of the world operate.

This evening we are sitting around that table with Jesus. He is not commenting about the guests of the prominent Pharisees or the host himself: He is commenting about us. He is saying, 'As you join in our meal, as you dine with Me, when did you last touch the untouchable? When did you last invite the undesirable? When did you last do the unthinkable? Well, if you've done it, then maybe you'll be blessed and you'll sit at that Messianic banquet at the end of time, enjoying the feast of eternity.

Radical Living
by Vinoth Ramachandra

Luke 18:15–29

The value of human life

What does it mean to be a human being? How do we gauge
the value and the worth of a human life? Those are questions
that lie at the heart of modern debates on abortion, genetic
engineering, ethnic cleansing and human rights. In the west-
ern philosophical tradition, great thinkers, as diverse as Plato
and Nietzsche have argued that human worth consists in
intellectual ability and physical fitness. Nietzsche went on to
sketch out a moral code encouraging physicians to cultivate
contempt for people who were chronically ill, or physically or
mentally deformed. The biblical teaching, therefore, that
human beings are made in the image of their Creator and
therefore from conception onwards are endowed with certain
rights, is unique and runs counter to the thinking of many of
our non-Christian friends and colleagues. That teaching was
unique in the ancient world. In traditional Asian cultures, as
well as in the classical Graeco-Roman world, some people
were considered superior to others. The value of a human life
consisted in what that life contributed to society. It was social

utility that determined human worth. So on the top social
rung there were rulers, politicians, philosophers, generals and
warriors – superior human beings. Lower down came people
who contributed materially to society, like artisans or farmers
or some slaves.

The value of children

What about children? Children often didn't come in at all. A
child had no intrinsic value or worth. A child's value was a
potential value. If this child developed into one of those superior adults, then he or she would have a value in society.
That was the thinking which forms the background to this
passage. It's why the disciples are shocked when they see Jesus
associating with toddlers brought to Him by their mothers.
They shared the thinking of their society. If Jesus was an
important man, then surely He should be associating with His
peers, with other important people. It was beneath His dignity
to be taking infants into His arms. So they rebuke Him, thinking that His values and priorities are all wrong; they think they
know better. But Jesus, in turn, rebukes them, saying, 'Let the
little children come to me, and do not hinder them, for the
kingdom of God belongs to such as these' (Lk. 18:16).

Now there are lots of sentimental things said about children
in some popular commentaries, with writers maintaining that
Jesus is pointing to the innocence, purity, or humility of children, or their simple trust. They look for some quality in a
child that fits them to be inheritors of the kingdom of God.
But I suggest that, if we keep that historical context in view,
what Jesus is pointing to is not some quality that children possess but rather the status that they do not possess. He is saying,
the kingdom of God is for people like little children who have
no status at all in society. It's for the nobodies, it's for the insig-
nificant people. After all, what do children possess? They don't
possess professional qualifications, wealth, or religious works
of merit. They possess nothing. And in the ancient world they
didn't even possess any legal status; you could do anything to a
child and the law wouldn't touch you. Infanticide was a very

common practice not just with mentally and physically deformed children, but even with physically healthy children who were unwanted, and very few voices were raised in protest. It was only the early church who began to rescue infants left to die on rubbish heaps outside Roman cities, and they did that because they took their cue from Jesus.

Then Jesus goes on to say something even more startling: 'Anyone who will not receive the kingdom of God like a little child will never enter it' (v. 17). There are two ways you can take this, both of which are inter-linked. *Firstly*, you receive the kingdom of God as you receive a little child. In other words, it is for people who show hospitality to those like little children – the nobodies of this world; who make a space for such people in their lives because Jesus comes to us in the form of the lame, the blind, the crippled, the lepers, the nobodies of this age. And so to receive such people is to receive God's kingdom. *Secondly*, unless you are prepared to become like a little child – a nobody in the eyes of society, you do not receive the kingdom of God. The kingdom of God is for those who are nobodies.

The rich young ruler

Now Luke goes on to record a story, in the verses immediately following, of a man who was unwilling to become a nobody, unwilling to become like a little child in that society. Verse 18, 'A certain ruler asked him, "Good teacher, what must I do to inherit eternal life?" "Why do you call me good?" Jesus answered. "No one is good – except God alone." ' Matthew calls him a young man and that could mean anything, in Jewish society, between twelve and forty. He is also a ruler, maybe of a Jewish synagogue, a position of great social standing, or even a member of the Jewish Sanhedrin – the parliament of Israel, an even higher ranking in society. Notice the language that the man uses. After Jesus has just been talking of receiving the kingdom of God as a little child, he asks, 'What must I do to inherit eternal life?' The Greek phrase literally means, 'the life of the age to come'. So while Jesus is speaking of receiving a gift, the man speaks of 'What must I do?' He calls Him 'Good teacher'. Perhaps, in his consciousness, he thinks of himself as basically a good, decent, upright, law-abiding citizen of high social rank in Israel coming to another man who is good and worthy of trust and respect and wanting a little religious advice. 'What more must I do that I might now inherit the life of the age to come?'

But Jesus deals with him rather abruptly, doesn't He? 'Why do you call me good? No one is good – except God alone.' Jesus is trying to get this man to stop and think about the language that he is using. Don't use words like goodness so glibly. If eternal life is life in the age to come, the age in which God will rule His universe where the whole creation will be filled with the presence of God, who can stand in the presence of such a God of awesome holiness and majesty? Or, if goodness is defined by the character of God, who amongst us can say that we are good? That we are like God? Think about those words that you use so rashly. He goes on, 'You know the commandments: do not commit adultery, do not murder, do not steal, do not give false testimony, honour your father and mother.' Jesus reminds him of the second half of Old Testament Law relating to our relationships with one another – the way we treat one another in human community. And the man says, 'All these I have kept since I was a boy.' When Jesus heard this, He said to him, 'You still lack one thing. Sell everything you have and give the money to the poor… Then come, follow me.' And Luke says, 'He became very sad.' In Matthew's version, 'He was shocked, and went away distressed' (cf. Mt. 19:22). Why? Because he had much wealth.

Money and spirituality

The man's reaction is a clue to his problem. In Luke's Gospel the disposition of our hearts towards God is always reflected in the disposition of our possessions. In other words, our spending patterns reflect our relationship with God. By putting His finger on this man's wealth, Jesus is trying to say to him: Look, there is a substitute for God in your life that you have not recognized. Jesus is the master communicator. If He had directly confronted the man with the question, 'Do you love God with all your heart, with all your soul, with all your strength?' the man would have said, like many of us, 'Yes, I do, at least I'm trying to.' In this indirect manner, Jesus gets him to see that there is something other than God at the centre of his affections and ambition: something that he cannot give up, even if God were to demand it. And that is his excessive wealth.

You could say this man has broken the first law, 'I am Yahweh your God, and you shall have no other gods besides Me.' And also the sixth law, 'You shall not steal.' In first-century Palestine, many people would have been extremely poor. For someone to have excessive wealth would have involved some historical theft, either on the part of this man, or on the part of his ancestors, some process of exploitation – maybe unjust prices given for the goods that he bought, or unfair wages for people who worked for him. Jesus is getting him to see that there is a God substitute, an idol in his life, and unless he is prepared to deal with it radically, he cannot become like a little child, he cannot receive the kingdom of God.

God substitutes

Augustine, the great fourth-century theologian, once said, 'All of us human beings stand in the presence of God with a clenched fist.' God wants to lavish His love and His goodness into our lives, but He has no place in which to put it because our fingers are locked around various 'God substitutes' – in this man's case it was his wealth. It may be even a spouse, work, ambition, a relationship that we cannot give up. And the only way that we can receive God's goodness is to unlock those tightly clasped fingers and come to God with an open hand, to receive. And that process is very painful. It's what the Bible calls repentance. The longer we have had our fingers clasped around objects or people or relationships, unable to yield them to God, the more painful is the process of repentance.

The great enemy – mammon

Today we are in danger of bowing to the idol of wealth. Again, in Luke's Gospel, this is a frequent theme: one of the great enemies of Christian discipleship is mammon. The Aramaic word *mammon* is a personification of money; it's more than just the wealth we have in our bank accounts, it's the spirit of acquisitiveness, of possessiveness, and of greed that drives the modern economy. That, says Jesus, is often the biggest hindrance to Christian discipleship.

Twenty-four-hour shopping is now available. Computer technology provides twenty-four hours of trading in commodities, speculation and foreign exchanges. Evangelical leaders face the danger of being seduced by the cult of celebrity, but perhaps more threatening is the cult of consumerism where shopping becomes an addiction. Shopping for things does not meet a physical or material need, but an emotional need. It's a form of identity construction. Why is it that people get into debt to buy Mercedes Benzes, or designer clothing, or to have that extra house in the country, or to send our children to some expensive private school? It is because these status symbols help us to construct our identity. We are like perpetual adolescents, always wanting to construct a new identity for ourselves. It is what we possess and consume that gives us our worth in the eyes of society. To parody the French philosopher Descartes, 'I eat and I drink therefore I am.'

I have here a £10 note. What is it that gives it its value? It is not the cost of the paper or the chemicals that have gone into its production. Who gave this paper its value of £10? Well, written on it is a promise from the chief cashier of the Bank of England: 'I promise to pay the bearer the sum of ten pounds' – a promise given by a human institution. It is we human beings who create the value of this money. I find it amusing that many hard-headed businessmen will say they live in the real world and have no time for religion, morality and ethics which get in the way of business. And yet this money is a product of promise keeping and promise keeping is about ethics. If we fail to honour our promises to one another, the whole economy grinds to a halt. What happens to this piece of paper? Remember it is we who have created it and given it value, but after a while, this piece of paper begins to control me. It decides what job I should have, who I should marry, where I should live, how many children I should have. It starts giving me my values. It tells me whom I should value in society, and whom I should not value. That is an example, if you like, of idol formation.

Behind every act of idol formation there is a prior act of forgetfulness. We forget who we are: God's creation made in His image. We forget that the things that we bow down and worship are things that we have created – they are inferior to us. Whether it is money, technology, families, political systems, or economic markets, these human creations now begin to enslave us and define who we are and we become their puppets. That is why, when society turns its back on God, it is not turning to some unbelief, not believing in nothing, it starts worshipping other gods. May I recommend my book about the formation and slavery of idols, *Gods that Fail*? That's the commercial break and an example of consumerism!

Let's get back to our passage.

The problem of riches

Jesus looks at the young ruler and says how hard it is for those who have wealth to enter the kingdom of God, 'It is easier for a camel to go through the eye of a needle than for someone who is rich to enter the kingdom of God' (v. 24). There are various ways in which rich Christians have tried to evade the bluntness of this teaching. In one popular commentary we read that what Jesus is saying here is not that it is impossible, it's just difficult. There was a gate in the city of Jerusalem in the time of Jesus called the 'eye of the needle' and if a camel wanted to go through that gate it had to get on its knees. So the rich can hold on to their possessions, providing they humble themselves before God. The only problem with that interpretation is that nobody has ever found a gate in Jerusalem called the 'eye of the needle': it's pure speculation. When we read Scripture, we try to evade the directness of the teaching of Jesus.

Those who heard it, including His disciples, asked, 'Who

then can be saved?' The disciples are thinking like the rest of their society that rich people, of great social standing, were also close to God. They had been blessed by God. That's why they were wealthy. It's what some of our very popular preachers say today – sickness and poverty are God's curse. If the rich cannot enter the kingdom of God, what chance have we, when we are always wanting to be like the rich! And so the disciples are perplexed by the words of Jesus. And Jesus says, 'What is impossible with men, is possible for God' (v. 27). In other words, every act of conversion of a rich man or woman is a sheer miracle. Conversion is about the rich becoming one with the poor, identifying with them and becoming their spokespersons in an act of social solidarity.

Our attitude to possessions

Then Peter says, 'We have left all we had to follow you.' And Jesus replies, 'I tell you the truth… no one who has left home or wife, or brothers or parents or children for the sake of the kingdom of God will fail to receive many times as much in this age and, in the age to come, eternal life.' Peter and the other disciples, the ones we call the twelve, had indeed left their homes and jobs to follow Jesus. But notice that there were other disciples in the Gospels who were not asked by Jesus to leave their homes or their jobs. Jesus is often in the home of Martha and Mary and their brother Lazarus. There are women who accompany the twelve and provide for them, including Jesus, out of their purses. So there seem to have been two kinds of disciples, both of equal value in the community of Jesus: those who sold their possessions and followed Jesus, and those who used their possessions, not for themselves, but for Jesus and the spread of the kingdom of God. In Acts 2, we read about the church in Jerusalem where many sold their estates and gave the money to the apostles to distribute amongst the poor. But we also know that the early Christians met in one another's homes. So clearly, some people kept their homes and used them for the wider family of God.

Perhaps this is the only way we can understand Jesus' words to the rich young ruler and this call upon our lives. We can have only two attitudes to our possessions if we call ourselves disciples of Jesus. Either we give up everything and live a life of voluntary poverty in following Jesus, or we radically rethink our attitudes to what we regard as our possessions: our brains, professional talents, homes, vehicles and bank accounts. These do not belong to us, they do not belong even to our children, they have been entrusted to us for the sake of the gospel. They belong to the wider family of Jesus Christ. They are to be tools used in the spread of the gospel and in serving the poor, the under-privileged and the needy in our midst.

Let me now develop certain themes that arise from this passage and are also prominent in other parts of Luke's Gospel.

The challenge to rethink the meaning of salvation

Jesus is speaking of receiving the kingdom of God: God's rule – His new order that has come into the world and is present in His ministry. The rich ruler asks Him a question about eternal life and the disciples ask, 'Who can be saved?' In the same passage you have these three different expressions: receiving or entering the kingdom of God, receiving eternal life and being saved. And it's clear that all three expressions refer to the same reality. But what is this one reality? What is salvation? Is salvation simply going to heaven when we die? That is how many evangelicals think of salvation. Nothing to do with this world.

How does Luke, in his Gospel, speak of salvation? Look at one example: Luke 1:46–47, Mary says: 'My soul praises the Lord and my spirit rejoices in God my Saviour.' The theme of God as Saviour is introduced and then, in verses 50–51, what are God's saving acts? 'His mercy extends to those who fear him, from generation to generation. He has performed mighty deeds with his arm; he has scattered those who are proud in their inmost thoughts.' This is what scholars call 'the prophetic present'. Mary is speaking of what God is going to do. His salvation is so imminent that she is speaking of it as if it had happened already. Verses 52–53, 'He has brought down rulers from their thrones but has lifted up the humble. He has filled the hungry with good things but has sent the rich away empty.' This is the language of political or at least social revolution. When God comes as Saviour this is what He will do and Jesus has been saying and demonstrating it in His ministry, in taking babies and toddlers into His arms and calling people to become like them. Whoever said that salvation has nothing to do with politics or economics? Of course salvation is more than economics and politics, but it cannot be less.

And the Bible ends with that wonderful picture, not of us going off to heaven but of heaven coming down to us. Of a new creation where God's presence fills every nook and cranny and He transforms it into what it was intended to be. So we read in Revelation 21 that there will be no more evil, no more tears no more pain, no more suffering, no more death. The things that have marred and spoiled the created order will now be no more. We shall see gathered before the throne of God people from all tribes and cultures and languages, worshipping God in their own tongues. We read of the kings of the earth bringing the glory and honour of all the cultures of the earth into the life of the kingdom of God. That speaks about the redemption of all cultures – everything that is good and beautiful and true, in every civilization on earth is not lost forever. It will be there redeemed and transformed to become a vehicle for the worship of God.

What a comprehensive vision of salvation. It's not simply private and individualistic and it gives your work a sense of dignity. If you are committed to developing that which is good and true and beautiful as an artist, a musician, an architect or a scientist, then that work is kingdom work because it contributes to the salvation of creation. So salvation has to do with the transforming of all our relationships: with God; with each other; with the non-human creation. And when God is truly God, only then will we be saved.

The challenge to rethink the meaning of the church

Gordon Fee describes the church as 'that company of people who live God's future in the present'. If what Mary has been singing about and the seer in the book of Revelation has been speaking about is true, that is our future – God's future, then we who have tasted the first fruits of that salvation are called to live God's priorities now. It's not that we bring about the kingdom of God by our own efforts, the kingdom of God is what the King brings. But we are called to be signs of that kingdom and so when we read, as Jesus in this passage says, that every need of the disciple community will be met, then He expects us to meet that need. When we read in the book of Revelation that He will wipe away every tear, there will be no more pain and suffering, it challenges us now in the present to work to alleviate human suffering, to resist evil, whatever form evil takes. And when we do that, whether in our local communities or on a global scale, we are pointing people to God's future; we are signs of His coming kingdom.

When we read of the peoples of the earth worshipping God in the multitude of languages, that should inspire us to world evangelization, to see the gospel proclaimed and translated into every culture. That vision of God's future, of God's salvation, inspires us to be God's church now, to be a sign of that coming new world.

The challenge to rethink the meaning of love

It's amazing that Jesus encounters a man who was sincere in searching for salvation and yet He seems to rebuff him. A man whom you and I would have gone out of out way to embrace and include in our church. Is it because Jesus doesn't love him as much as we do? Mark tells us, 'He looked at him and loved him' (Mk. 10:21). Then He says, 'Sell everything you have and give to the poor… then come, follow me' (v. 22). I find that very disturbing because it challenges my understanding of love.

The way to be popular with people, to be a nice guy, is to be like them, to say things they like to hear; Jesus was not a nice guy. Not because He tried to be deliberately unpopular or offensive, but because, as we have seen, the kingdom that

He proclaimed was an upside-down kingdom, where those at the bottom of the heap will be exalted and those at the top of the social ladder will be brought down. In that kingdom all false values and false gods are exposed and unless we are willing to expose the false values and the false gods in people's lives, we don't truly love them. Jesus can put His finger on the one thing in this man's life that is a hindrance to the knowledge of God. And so must we if we truly love our friends, our neighbours or even the stranger. We need to pray for discernment and ask God to help us in the way Jesus did, often not confrontationally but indirectly, bringing them to a point where they can see what god they are really worshipping in the place of the living and true Creator.

I also ask myself, what kind of friend would I like? Do I want a friend who is always nice to me, always affirming me, always telling me what I like to hear? Or do I want a friend who has the courage to tell me this is the idol you are enslaved to – you need to give it up? I pray that you and I will have friends like that: friends like Jesus.

Jonah 4
by Vaughan Roberts

Imagine the scene. Billy Graham is back at home in the States having just returned from Baghdad and he is furious. Two days before, he had been preaching in the great city of Baghdad, and thousands had turned up to hear him. Even Saddam Hussein was there. Those who couldn't get into the stadium were listening on the radio, or watching on TV – totally gripped by the message. At the end of his talk those who wanted to receive Christ got out of their seats, even Saddam. The phone lines were completely jammed. The whole city was converted. And yet Billy is in America, livid, and shouting at God, 'Why did you have to go and save that lot? Don't you know who they are, these dreadful Iraqis? Don't you know what kind of lives they live?' It is an inconceivable scene, isn't it? Billy Graham and the whole Christian world would not be angry if Baghdad was converted; surely we would be rejoicing in such a remarkable miracle.

We find it hard to relate to Jonah in chapter 4. You remember the story so far. Jonah was a prophet of God, sent with a message from God, to Nineveh, a city in Assyria, the great enemy of Israel at that time. Not wanting to go, he ran away in the opposite direction, got on board a ship and fled from God. There was a storm. The hard-nosed sailors were terrified and came to the conclusion that God must be angry with someone on board. They cast lots and the lot fell on Jonah. He wasn't surprised. He knew God was angry with him. With resignation and considerable courage he said, 'Throw me overboard and then you will be safe.' They did and they were. The sea was completely calm. Jonah must have thought that was the end, but God, in His mercy, hadn't finished with him. He sent a great fish to swallow him up. He was inside the fish for three days and three nights, after which it vomited him on to the shore. God had saved him.

Then the command came again, 'Go to Nineveh.' And this time Jonah went, with remarkable results. He simply proclaimed God's Word. 'Forty more days and Nineveh will be overturned.' And the Ninevites believed the message, turned urgently to God, repenting of their sin and pleading for mercy. In His grace God relented and the threatened destruction of their city did not occur. It's a miracle as remarkable as the whole of Baghdad being converted. Surely, if we were Jonah, we would have been overjoyed, wouldn't we? But he wasn't. He was very angry indeed.

As we read Jonah 4, it is hard to identify with him and see what relevance these verses might have for us. We can identify with Jonah running away from God; we've done that often. We can even identify with him in the belly of that fish. We too, before we turned to Christ, were helpless, under the judgement of God – in the sea of God's wrath. We are with Jonah all the way until now. His behaviour here is so outrageous it is inconceivable that we could do anything similar. How could he be angry after God had rescued the whole of Nineveh through his preaching? Can I suggest to you that we are not as different from Jonah as we like to think. There is a lot of Jonah in each of us.

Jonah's anger (4:1–3)

'But Jonah was greatly displeased and became angry. He prayed to the Lord' (vv. 1–2). Compare this with the prayer that Jonah prayed from inside the fish when he was a chastened man (ch. 2). Aware of his sin in running away from God and of God's righteous judgement, he prayed for mercy. The first prayer, in chapter 2, is prayed in humility, but the second, in chapter 4, is prayed in pride. In the first, he emptied himself and in the second, he is full of himself. In the first, he was justifying God and accusing himself, but in the second, he is justifying himself and accusing God. This prayer is all about I and Me and My. Those words appear six times in the NIV, nine times in the original Hebrew.

He had been forgiven for the sin of refusing God's commission to preach to Nineveh. He had been rescued from death in the sea and delivered on the dry land just days before, yet here we find him justifying his sin. How could the chastened Jonah of chapter 2, humbled by the grace of God, full of gratitude to Him, turn so quickly into the proud, bitter, self-obsessed man of chapter 4? We do seem to be back to square one. Had that spiritual revival that came to him after God had saved him meant nothing?

Before we condemn him too quickly, before we express incredulity at his behaviour, we need to face some uncomfortable facts. Like Jonah, those who trust in Christ have experienced an amazing rescue. We too were at the bottom of a deep pit, cut off from God, because of our sins. And yet amazingly, because of the death and resurrection of Christ, those of us who have trusted in Him have been raised from that pit and are enjoying new life in Christ, friendship with God. For a time, like Jonah in chapter 2, we are full of praise and gratitude. We sing, 'Amazing Grace, how sweet the sound that saved a wretch like me.' But that experience of being rescued from God's judgement does not take away the sin in our hearts. It's possible to be on a spiritual high one day, praising from our hearts the God who has rescued us, and the next day fighting against that same God and resisting His will for our lives. We can go from great highs to terrible lows; that's the kind of people we are and so it's not impossible to imagine what is happening to Jonah between chapter 2 and chapter 4. It happens to us. We have received the Spirit of God, but the sinful nature still remains and drags us down. Let's not delude ourselves: we may have received God's rescue, but we are still capable of sinking into terrible rebellion against Him. And that applies to all of us. It can even happen to great preachers, sadly, like Jonah.

Perhaps we say, OK, I can see that I am like Jonah, I can fall back into rebellion against God, but I simply cannot see that I am like him in his anger over God rescuing others. I cannot imagine myself doing that. And that does seem to be why Jonah was angry. He'd suspected, all along, that God would have mercy on the people of Nineveh. He says, 'That is why I was so quick to flee to Tarshish. I knew you were a gracious and compassionate God, slow to anger and abounding in love' (v. 2). He even says, in verse 3, 'I'd be better off dead.' This is no passing mood; it is deep spiritual depression.

There have been a number of attempts to explain Jonah's anger. I want to suggest that in his heart he is battling against a great truth that this book communicates above all others: 'Salvation comes from the Lord' (2:9). God is in complete control of the universe: He has power over the wind and the sea, He can even summon a fish to do His work, He does what He wants, when He wants, how He wants. There is no greater power to whom God is beholden. He alone takes the initiative in salvation. He is the God of sovereign mercy, as the sailors discovered in chapter 1; God saved them from the storm. Jonah discovered that in chapter 2; God saved him from the sea. And the Ninevites discovered it in chapter 3; God saved them from destruction. But in chapter 4 we find Jonah resenting God's sovereign mercy on the people of Nineveh.

If you like, God has two hands: a hand of judgement, which He uses when He punishes sin, and a hand of mercy, which He uses when He forgives sin. Jonah is angry because God, in his mind at least, had used the wrong hand in His dealings with Nineveh. As far as he is concerned, God should have used the hand of judgement, not the hand of mercy. Maybe he was motivated by a concern for his own reputation as a prophet. He prophesied the destruction of Nineveh in forty days, but it didn't happen. God relented. How did that make Jonah look? Perhaps some would even accuse him of being a false prophet. But actually there is no hint in the passage that that was the concern in Jonah's mind. I suspect his anger was not as rational as that. If we'd talked to him in his sober

moments, I'm sure we would have found that his theology
was absolutely orthodox. He knew God was sovereign and
could do what He liked. He knew that His loving concern for
himself and the people of Israel was all of grace. His rescue
from that fish was just as undeserved as the mercy God
showed to the Ninevites. Sadly, as so often is the case in our
lives, his heart was a long way away from his mind. He knew
in his mind that God was sovereign, but in his heart he still
had God all boxed up.

There were certain people who were outside the confines
of God's mercy, possibly all Gentiles – all non-Jews, certainly
those dreadful Ninevites who were known for their depravity,
the great enemies of Israel. Very likely it wasn't just racism that
motivated Jonah's anger, it was a warped sense of moral indig-
nation. How could a holy God possibly forgive such wicked
people? Surely justice demanded that He punish them? So
maybe Jonah was not concerned for his reputation but for
God's. What would people think of a God who let such evil
people off scot-free? His problem was with God's sovereign
mercy – His grace.

This book falls neatly into two halves. The first two chapters focus on God's mercy to Jonah and the next two on God's
mercy to Nineveh. In chapter 2 we find Jonah's response to
God's grace shown to him – he is full of praise inside the fish.
In chapter 4 we find Jonah's response to God's grace shown to
the Ninevites and this time, he is full of anger. That is totally
inconsistent. He had forgotten how undeserving he and all
the people of Israel were. He took God's grace to them for
granted, but resented it when it was shown to others. He'd
forgotten the lessons that he had seemed to have learned
inside the fish. He couldn't see that he stood in the same place
as those Ninevites, as a sinner deserving nothing but God's
destruction. He had no compassion on them, no desire that
they should be saved. They could go to hell for all he cared.
God's justice demanded such a punishment for people like
that.

Now that we have begun to understand Jonah's anger a
little, I wonder if we can see how like him we are. In our
heads we believe all the right things. We know God is

sovereign in the exercise of His mercy. We know we deserve it no more than anyone else. But how easy it is to take that mercy for granted and to cease to identify with those outside it. We are concerned for some of them, those we like, who belong to our group or type. But if we are honest, we have very little concern for many of the others. If God deals with them with the hand of judgement, so be it, that's what they deserve anyway. We can all think of people we don't find it easy to relate to: that critical boss at work, that judgemental neighbour, or perhaps that group of people. Sadly, racism, snobbery or inverse snobbery are never far from us, even if they are subconscious. We box God in. We want Him to exercise His mercy on those we long to see saved, but others we consign quite happily to His hand of judgement. We show we are more like Jonah than we care to admit. We too need to learn.

God's lesson (4:4–11)

Isn't verse 4 encouraging? Jonah is furious with God, but God doesn't tell him off for expressing his anger. There are times when, like Jonah, we are perplexed. We cannot understand what God is doing in our lives or the lives of our loved ones or just in the world around us. We want to shout at God, 'What are you playing at?' But a false piety tell us that is wrong. We mustn't speak our mind to God; we have got to get our hearts right before we can present them to Him. What folly! He is a God who sees right into our hearts. Nothing is hidden from Him, so we might as well express what we are feeling to Him in prayer. The Psalms express what is really going on inside and that is what Jonah does. He came to God as he was and was not met with a rebuke. I praise God for that. God, in His loving patience, takes him as he is and tries to teach him a lesson. So He asks him, 'Jonah, have you any right to be angry?' Jonah is silent (v. 5), he simply leaves the city, sets up camp and waits to see what will happen. Perhaps God would come to His senses and destroy Nineveh after all.

The scene is now set for God's lesson. Jonah had been

unable to accept God's exclusive right to have 'mercy on whom He will have mercy' and so God provided a visual aid to illustrate His sovereignty. It was a hot climate and Jonah would have been uncomfortable even in his shelter. Then, verse 6, God miraculously accelerated the growth of a vine which provided extra shade. And not suprisingly, we read that 'Jonah was very happy about that vine'. He possibly saw it as divine confirmation that at last God had come round to his way of thinking. If so, his hopes were soon dashed. Look at verse 7, 'But at dawn the next day God provided a worm, which chewed the vine so that it withered.' Once more we see the mighty Creator directing nature to do His will. And then, to make matters worse, God summoned a scorching wind which, combined with the relentless blaze of the sun, made Jonah feel terrible! Again he says, 'It would be better for me to die than to live' (v. 8). God responded with the same question that he posed after Jonah's last death wish. 'Do you have a right to be angry about the vine?' 'I do,' he said. 'I'm angry enough to die.' The words of a stubborn child. His self-confidence still isn't shaken. He is convinced that he is right about Nineveh and God is wrong; the city should be judged. And he is equally convinced that God is wrong in the way He has treated him by callously taking away that vine.

Jonah still hadn't learnt his lesson. He will not let God be God. In the last two verses God points out how foolish and small-minded he is being. He draws a contrast between the plant and the people of Nineveh. 'But the Lord said, "You have been concerned about this vine, though you did not tend it or make it grow. It sprang up overnight and died overnight. But Nineveh has more than a hundred and twenty thousand people who cannot tell their right hand from their left and many cattle as well. Should I not be concerned about that great city?"' (vv. 10–11).

'Jonah, you didn't make that vine or sustain it. You only knew it for one day and yet you were very upset when it was destroyed. I can understand that,' says God. 'But can't you understand Me when I feel for the thousands of people of Nineveh whom I created and have sustained for years? They aren't just plants – here today and gone tomorrow – they are people, human beings with eternal destinies. Should I not be concerned about that great city?' And that is where the book ends.

In many ways it is an unsatisfactory ending. It's left hanging in the air. We are deliberately not told how Jonah responds. Just imagine there was a verse 12 which read like this: 'Jonah replied, "Yes Lord, of course you should be concerned for them and so should I." He left his shelter and went back to the city where he rejoiced with all the people at the salvation they had received from God.' If the book ended like that we would be left with a nice warm glow, wouldn't we? Good old Jonah, he's come round in the end. And they all lived happily ever after.

We are not meant to be reassured by this book. It is designed to leave us uncomfortable, with that final question ringing in our ears, 'Should I not be concerned about that great city?' and with the implied question burning in our hearts – should we not be concerned as well? The book of Jonah has presented us with a portrait of a sovereign God, who has power over everything: the wind, the sea, the fish, the vine. But above all, a God who is sovereign in mercy, a God who refuses to be boxed in, who refuses to show His love only to those we regard as kosher. His mercy extends to all: to the Israelite prophet, the pagan sailors and those wicked Ninevites. They deserved God's judgement, but so did Jonah and he had no right to resent God's mercy to others.

These four chapters present a powerful challenge, in their original context, to that self-satisfied, xenophobic nation of Israel who were meant to be God's light to the Gentiles and the nations. But they kept the love of God to themselves and they scorned the nations. They were expecting the Day of the Lord to come and bring judgement to others. They didn't deserve the mercy of God. Like Jonah, they couldn't wait for judgement to come on those foreigners. Their callous indifference showed that their hearts were a long way from God's. He 'rejoices over every sinner that repents'.

How do we fare when we compare ourselves to God?

Aren't we far more like Jonah? We may not have an out-burst of anger when we hear reports of a great revival some-where; we show our lack of compassion in more subtle ways. Of course we want the teenager off that rough estate or the student from overseas to come to know Christ, but we won't talk with him, after all, we have so little in com-mon. And to be honest it is just such hard work talking to people from other backgrounds and cultures. We want non-churchgoers to be converted, but we don't think about going to them; we expect them to come to us, resenting any minor changes that we need to make in our services to accommodate them. We have always met at 9 a.m., surely they ought to be out of bed by then! The language we use in our services is a bit old fashioned, but other people should take us as they find us. Oh yes, we believe in evan-gelism in theory, but when it comes to the crunch, we pre-fer our church to be a cosy club for insiders, we don't want the trouble of trying to reach those outside.

I don't think we really realize what a crisis there is in our country. We come to Keswick and the tent is full and we think things are going pretty well, but the vast majority of people in Britain are growing up without any touch of the gospel or of Christian people. It is just another world to them.

How are we going to reach our nation? Are we just going to expect them to come to us on our terms? We won't reach people that way. It's time we woke up and had some real compassion for those out of touch with the gospel of Christ. And real compassion means sacrifice, not some pious plati-tude, 'Lord save them.' It means our churches actually doing something, not simply inviting them to come to us, but going to them. My longing is that we will see church plants going up all around the country as we go to where they are and try to fit in with them as culturally as possible. The only thing that mustn't change is the gospel; *we* are to adapt.

The situation may be desperate at home, but what about other countries and cultures throughout the world, where few know about Christ? We say we care, but do we? Do we care enough to pray passionately? Do we care enough to give sacrificially? Do we care enough to go? Of course in our heads we want to see them saved and trusting in Christ, what about our hearts? God says, 'Should I not be concerned about that great city?' Of course He should. What about us? Should we not be concerned as well?

Keswick 2000
Tapes, Videos and Books

Catalogues and price lists of audio tapes of the Keswick Convention platform ministry, including much not included in the present book, can be obtained from:

The Administrator
The Convention Office
PO Box 105
Uckfield
East Sussex
TN22 5GY
Tel: 01435 866034
E-mail: office@keswickconv.com

Details of videos of selected sessions can be obtained from:

Mr Dave Armstrong
STV Videos
Box 299
Bromley
Kent
BR2 9XB

Some previous annual Keswick volumes (all published by STL/OM) are still in print and can be ordered from:

The Keswick Convention Centre, Skiddaw Street, Keswick, Cumbria, CA12 4BY;

from your local Christian bookseller;

or direct from the publishers, OM Publishing, STL Ltd, PO Box 300, Carlisle, Cumbria CA3 0QS, England

Keswick 2001

The annual Keswick Convention takes place in the heart of England's beautiful Lake District. It offers an unparalleled opportunity for listening to gifted Bible exposition, experiencing Christian fellowship with believers from all over the world, and enjoying something of the unspoilt grandeur of God's creation. Each of the weeks has a series of morning Bible Readings, followed by other addresses throughout the rest of the day. There are also regular meetings for young people and a Children's Holiday Club.

The dates for Keswick 2001 (which will run for **3** weeks) are:

Week 1 – July 14–20   Bible Readings by Bishop Michael Baughen
                            Other Speakers: Joel Edwards, Charles Price, Frank Retief

Week 2 – July 21–27   Bible Readings by Rev. Stephen Gaukroger
                            Other Speakers: Paul Negrut
                            (The rest to be confirmed)

Week 3 – July 28-Aug 2   (note this period ends on a Thursday)
                            Bible Readings by Rev. Stuart Briscoe
                            Other Speakers: Jill Briscoe, Paul Weston, Dave Bourke

For further information contact:

The Administrator
The Convention Office
PO Box 105
Uckfield
East Sussex
TN22 5GY
Tel: 01435 866034
E-mail: office@keswickconv.com

Appendix

Changes in the Keswick Convention Council

Jonathan Lamb, who has served as the Convention Council Chairman since 1996, stepped down from this position at the 2000 Convention and his replacement is Peter Maiden – Associate International Co-ordinator for Operation Mobilisation.

New to the Council this year: Tricia Lee, an office administrator; Joanne Good of the Africa Inland Mission; Ian Randall, lecturer at Spurgeon's College and the International Baptist Seminary in Prague; and Rev. Ian Wright, Vicar of Bassenthwaite, who serves as a local representative.